WITHDR

BEING ME WITH OCD

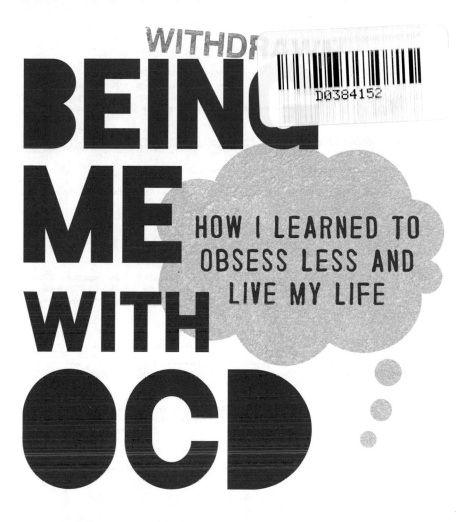

HOW I LEARNED TO OBSESS LESS AND LIVE MY LIFE

ALISON DOTSON

FOREWORD BY ELIZABETH MCINGVALE

free spirit
PUBLISHING®

Library of Congress Cataloging-in-Publication Data
Dotson, Alison.
    Being me with OCD : how I learned to obsess less and live my life / Alison Dotson ; foreword by Elizabeth McIngvale.
        pages cm
    Audience: Age 15 and older.
    Includes bibliographical references and index.
    ISBN-13: 978-1-57542-470-5
    ISBN-10: 1-57542-470-3
1. Obsessive-compulsive disorder in adolescence—Patients—Anecdotes. 2. Obsessive-compulsive disorder in adolescence—Treatment. 3. Teenagers—Mental Health. I. Title. II. Title: Being me with obsessive-compulsive disorder.
    RJ506.O25.D68 2014
    616.85'22700835—dc23

                                                                                        2013044768
eBook ISBN: 978-1-57542-637-2

The concepts, ideas, and suggestions contained in this book are not intended as substitutes for professional healthcare.

This book was typeset and designed using the following freeware or open license typefaces:
Candela © "Joan Alegret" and "La Tipomatika" • tipomatika.co.nr
Blackout © www.theleagueofmoveabletype.com
Charis SIL © scripts.sil.org/cms/scripts/page.php?site_id=nrsi&cat_id=Home

Cover and interior design by Tasha Kenyon
Edited by Eric Braun and Marjorie Lisovskis

Reading Level High School–Adult; Interest Level Ages 15 & Up
Fountas & Pinnell Guided Reading Level Z+

10 9 8 7 6 5 4 3 2
Printed in the United States of America
S18860214

Free Spirit Publishing Inc.
Minneapolis, MN
(612) 338-2068
help4kids@freespirit.com
www.freespirit.com

For Peter: You've loved me as deeply in my darkest moments as in our shared moments of joy.

For Mom and Dad: The Fates conspired to give me two of the most loving, compassionate, and understanding people as my parents. I am me because I have you.

READ THIS FIRST

This book is about my personal experience with OCD (obsessive compulsive disorder), from my confusion to my diagnosis to my eventual triumph. I've had OCD for so long, and have read so much about it since being diagnosed several years ago, that sometimes I feel like I know everything there is to know about the disorder. I've become comfortable talking about my own experience, answering any questions people might have, and listening to others who are struggling.

However, I'm not an expert. I am simply a person who suffered from OCD for years and years, and I suffered enough that I want to help others who are in pain. When I was diagnosed at age 26 I was in a really low place. I took the advice of my doctor—I took prescribed medication and read the books he recommended, which outlined steps to take toward recovery and included successful case studies of people who never thought they'd get better. I share all of that in greater detail in the pages of this book. My hope is that you're inspired by my story and know that no matter how low you're feeling now you can still get better. Maybe some of the coping techniques that worked for me will work for you, too.

The book was carefully reviewed by a psychiatrist and a psychologist, both specialists in anxiety disorders, so I could feel completely confident about the information and suggestions I've included. But my story and the advice I share are not intended to replace medical expertise. This book is meant only as a complement to professional help.

CONTENTS

FOREWORD

by Elizabeth McIngvale, LMSW

At the age of 12 my life was turned upside down. I found myself overcome by obsessive thoughts. I worried so much about keeping my family members safe and many other things that I constantly engaged in rituals in an attempt to keep these obsessions at bay. I tried to hide my rituals because, like Alison Dotson, I was ashamed of my behavior. I was lost, scared, and alone.

Soon, I could no longer conceal what was going on, and I broke down and explained it all to my mom. With her help, I learned that I was living with obsessive-compulsive disorder, or OCD. Fast-forward three years later, and OCD had taken over my life. My OCD centered around scrupulosity (the religious form of OCD), contamination, color and number issues, and hyper-responsibility. I often got stuck in rituals such as washing or walking and re-walking over certain areas in my house. My rituals soon took up the majority of my days, and I was no longer the carefree girl everyone knew from three years before. I was homebound by this illness and couldn't find the help I needed.

Eventually, my parents found an inpatient clinic that specialized in OCD. Shortly after my 15th birthday, I was checked into this clinic, and once again my life was turned upside down—this time for the better. I learned how to successfully manage my OCD with cognitive behavioral therapy, specifically exposure and response prevention (the gold standard for OCD treatment). With hard work and dedication, I was able to regain my life and diminish my OCD symptoms. I was no longer scared and alone—I was hopeful and determined to manage my OCD.

Although I continue to live with OCD and have had ups and downs along the way, I now have the tools I need to manage my illness. Some days are harder than others, but I know I can live the life that I deserve to live by continuing my exposures with response (ritual) prevention. My experiences have inspired me to help others with this illness. Like Alison has done by sharing her story in this book, I have spoken publicly about my struggles with OCD and have opened my life for others to see. Sharing my story can be very difficult, but it has been well worth it if I have helped even one person.

As someone who, like me, has hit rock bottom and fought her way back up, Alison shares my dedication to helping others. In *Being Me with OCD*, you will find stories that may ring true to your experiences, stories that are surprising, sad, and heartbreakingly funny. You will find words of encouragement, tools to help you get through the day, a collection of helpful resources, and one important, life-affirming message: You are not alone. There is help.

In my work at the International OCD Foundation, the Peace of Mind Foundation, and the OCD Challenge, I am inspired time and time again by the stories of others who live with OCD. Telling your story is never easy, but I have seen the power of these stories to help others find the strength to fight their own OCD. I hope you will find hope and inspiration in Alison's story. I commend her for her courage and devotion to helping others living with obsessive-compulsive disorder.

Even after therapists told my family that my OCD was too severe to be treated, I found the help that I needed. My life was changed forever. No matter how hopeless you might feel at times, you can do the same. There is help, and there is hope.

Elizabeth McIngvale
Spokesperson for the International OCD Foundation
Founder of the Peace of Mind Foundation

CLIMBING UP FROM ROCK BOTTOM

> "Pain of mind is worse than pain of body."
>
> —Publius Syrus

In my mid-20s I worked as a proofreader at a small graphic design firm. One day, I sat in my office with the sliding door pulled shut, holding my head in my hands, trying to use them as blinders against distractions.

I tried to force myself to concentrate, to keep proofreading and absorb what I was reading and not let an obsessive thought enter my mind. Instead, as usual, a fleeting but disgustingly graphic image appeared, an image that was so wrong and unwelcome that my stomach twisted. I clenched my fingers around my red pen as tears welled up in my eyes.

I was crying—again. At work. And anyone could witness it; all they had to do was knock on my door or open it and walk right in, and they would see me sitting at my desk crying, my face pink and streaked with tears. I couldn't let that happen because there was no way I could explain myself. So instead I composed myself as much as possible, walked through the office, and hurried down the main hall toward the bathroom, willing myself to keep it together for just a few seconds longer. I passed a woman from another office and I stretched a fake smile across my face, hoping she couldn't actually *see* the lump sitting so heavily in my throat.

I rounded the corner, pushed through the doorway to the stairwell, let out a single sob as I rushed down the stairs, quickly composed myself again, just in case, and then locked myself in a bathroom stall, where I collapsed on the toilet seat into a snotty, convulsing heap. I let myself cry, giving it everything I had, trying to get it out of my system so I could go back to work and finish out the day. After a few minutes I blew my nose one more time, left the stall, and splashed cold water on my face.

This had become my life: I had had obsessions for as long as I could remember, and this wasn't the first time I had been depressed. But it was the first time I struggled so much with getting through each day. And it was the first time I seriously considered suicide.

I had hit rock bottom.

I didn't know I had a treatable disorder called obsessive-compulsive disorder (OCD). All I knew was that I had been plagued with unsettling, disturbing, and *very* unwanted thoughts off and on for years: In middle school and high school I obsessed over the idea that I might be gay; in college I had religious obsessions that made me think I was destined for eternal punishment; and now, as an adult, I couldn't shake the terrible fear that I would sexually assault someone—a relative, a child, a stranger, anyone I wasn't *supposed* to touch.

Somehow, though, I got out of bed every morning and went to work. I went through all of the day-to-day motions. When I became eligible to enroll in my company's 401(k) plan, I received a phone call from a retirement advisor. I listened to him talk about how important it was to save for the future, and I answered all his questions. *(If someone gave you 50 dollars for your birthday, would you spend it all, or save it all, or somewhere in the middle? If you had a retirement savings account, would you want access to it, or would you wait until you retired to withdraw any money?)*

I wanted to end the conversation, explain to the nice man that I didn't really care. I couldn't imagine living a few more months, let alone several more decades. It was overwhelming to even try.

If you're reading this book you've probably obsessed, too, and maybe you've performed compulsions so you can feel better, if only temporarily. Or maybe someone you care about has these symptoms, and you want to understand what that person is going through, or you want to help.

You're not alone: In the United States, about 1 in 100 adults and 1 in 200 kids have OCD. Other people have obsessed as you have obsessed and performed compulsions just as you have. Some people (like me) have what is called "pure O," meaning they obsess but don't perform compulsions. Others have obsessions and engage in compulsive behavior in an attempt to ward off their fears or prevent bad things from happening.

Compulsions are easier to see than obsessions, so people often associate OCD with a person who washes his hands a lot or with someone whose house is always *just so*. It's hard to know exactly how many people have "taboo" obsessions, because they often feel too ashamed to tell anyone, and it goes unnoticed.

And that's a big problem. It can take years for someone with OCD to get the right help, and not because psychiatrists and therapists don't know what to do. Rather, it's because we *don't seek it out.* I was so sure I would be judged that I didn't make an appointment with a psychiatrist until I was 26 years old—and I had been obsessing for well over a decade.

I might not have gotten any help at all if I hadn't found an article that gave me hope. Something told me I was *obsessing,* and I'd been looking up the word *obsession* in my work dictionary several times a day, reading and re-reading "compulsive preoccupation with a fixed idea or an unwanted feeling or emotion." From there I researched OCD online and began to piece things together. Eventually I found the website for the International OCD Foundation, and an article called "Thinking Bad Thoughts." It wasn't written for me; rather, it was a piece for therapists who wanted to help their patients who had sexual obsessions. Fascinated and encouraged, I scrolled through the pages, reading about people who close or cross their legs in public to prevent inappropriate behavior, about therapy for adults who fear they will molest a child, about helping people face their worst fears.

The authors of "Thinking Bad Thoughts" didn't judge their patients. They didn't worry that these people were dangerous or perverted or capable of bringing harm to anyone. Instead, it was clear that OCD was the culprit and that therapy offered proven treatment methods.

For the first time in several months I felt lighter. Hopeful.

That night I went out to see a Neil Diamond tribute band and I actually had a great time. (There was something so endearing about a big college-age guy swaying in time and passionately belting out "Sweet Caroline," a ballad even older than he was.) When I looked around the room at other people, I didn't feel jealous that they were "normal" and I wasn't, like I usually did when I saw people having fun; I watched them laugh and smile and dance and felt that soon enough I could do all those things without a weight on my shoulders and in my gut.

I wrote this book because I don't want you to wait to get help, like I did, because you're ashamed or you think nobody will understand. It was only after I'd learned others had gone through what I was going through that I realized I wasn't a monster or a deviant. I had a problem that had a name and a solution.

I wrote this book because I want you to have a resource meant just for you, more than a scholarly article written by a therapist for therapists.

Mostly, I wrote this book to help you find the courage and support you need to get help. That means finding a caring professional who can meet your unique needs, books that will really speak to you, and a community of like-minded peers.

I have had OCD for at least 20 years—maybe more. I've shared my deepest secrets with a psychiatrist, taken medication, dealt with social stigma, and done many of the everyday things you're doing while experiencing OCD symptoms, like going to school, dating, and holding a job. I'm not a doctor or mental-health expert. I'm just a regular person with OCD, a person who wanted to live a fuller life. Armed with the knowledge and compassion of my psychiatrist, information in books by OCD professionals, and therapeutic techniques, I have pulled myself up from rock bottom. This book is the story of my journey. You'll get a glimpse into some of the most personal and gut-wrenching experiences of my life, moments I've never shared with anyone else—not my husband, not my mom, not my best friend. I'm sharing them now because I hate the idea that others are hurting the way I was. It's my hope that by reading how I began to save myself—with help from others—you will see how you can do the same.

But this book is more than just a story. It's also full of practical tools and resources you can use to help yourself—like how to venture into exposure and response prevention on your own (see page 65) and how to find the right doctor—as well as advice and reassurance that you can do it. And, because I'm only one person with my own experience, this book also contains the personal stories of eight teens and young adults, in their own words. (These stories are real, although in some cases the names have been changed for privacy reasons.) Kiersten (see page 73) was anguished as she struggled to find the right medicine for her OCD. Rachel (see page 91) checked herself into a residential treatment program to tackle her symptoms. Robert (see page 61) underwent exposure and response prevention sessions (see page 60 for more information). All these stories are unique, just like your own, and together they shed light on the many ways OCD manifests itself, how many treatment options there are, and how a strong support system and a positive attitude can go a long way toward helping you feel better.

Today, I still have bad thoughts, but I know how to deal with them. When I look back on the years of suffering I went through, I wish I could talk to that tormented person I was. If I could, I would tell her she was not a bad person. I would tell her that her obsessions did not define her—and I would tell her to hurry up and make an appointment with a professional who could help! Since I can't do that, I am telling you. You have the power to face your fears, to take them down a peg and put them in their place. Getting better won't always be easy, but it will be worth it. And I will cheer you on every step of the way.

I would love to hear from you, wherever you are in your journey. Let's keep learning from each other and building each other up.

Write to me in care of my publisher at help4kids@freespirit.com.

Alison Dotson

CHAPTER 1
OCD AND ME

"'I am not OCD. OCD is not me.' This way of thinking was foundational to my strategy in defeating OCD."

—Shannon Shy, author of *It'll Be Okay:*
How I Kept Obsessive-Compulsive Disorder
(OCD) from Ruining My Life

I grew up in a safe and loving home with trusting, understanding, and warm parents, two older brothers, and a West Highland white terrier named McDuff or, less formally, Duffer. Mine was a comfortable existence, maybe even sheltered. I realized early on that not everyone's life was as carefree as mine, and it didn't sit well with me. How could I be so lucky while others suffered? It seemed to be only a matter of time before my luck ran out, that my life would take a turn for the worse. Irrational fears began to take over.

When I read *Deenie,* a Judy Blume novel about a teenage girl with scoliosis, I lay awake for several nights, convinced I had scoliosis, too, and would have to wear a cumbersome back brace, just as Deenie had. I pressed my back into the floor to see how straight my spine felt, and I tried to examine my back in my vanity mirror.

When I saw *The Ann Jillian Story,* a TV movie about an actress who survived breast cancer, I believed I must also have a cancerous tumor. Over and over I imagined myself poking a dinner fork through my flesh and pulling the growth out. I would lie in my bed and cry, asking God why I had to have breast cancer, why I had to die. One day, worried about me locked away in my bedroom at the end of the hall, my mom knocked on my door. Not wanting to devastate her with my "news," I pulled myself together and opened the door a crack. "Are you okay?" she asked. I nodded numbly and told her it was my stomach—again. After she left, I stood at my bedroom window, watching my brothers, dad, and dog play in the front yard. Duffer was running around in joyful circles, over and over again, and I choked up, thinking, "He's so full of life." I felt incredibly jealous.

And, perhaps most terrifying, when I watched a TV movie about a boy whose father had set him on fire during a custody dispute, I believed I was destined to be horribly marred in a fire. I would sob in bed at night, begging God to reconsider. Before bed I'd inspect my heating vents, making sure there weren't pieces of paper or T-shirts covering them.

Every time I thought I was over one fear, a new fear managed to weasel its way into my psyche, making it nearly impossible to sleep or concentrate.

Despite all of these horrifying images and irrational destinies I imagined for myself, I never told a soul. I never let anyone see me cry, and if they happened to, I lied about why I was crying. If only I had told my mom something, anything. She would have pulled me onto her lap and held me close, telling me not to be afraid. Maybe she would have helped me see that the things I feared were baseless. Maybe she would have helped me work through my fears—my obsessions—so they didn't have so much control over me.

But I kept it all inside. Every panic-inducing fear I faced for nearly 20 years, I faced alone. Not because I had to. But, rather, because I somehow understood that as terrifying as these persistent and intrusive fears were, they weren't *normal*. They were so heavy. They felt insurmountable. What could anyone do to help me? What was the point in sharing my fears?

I was like a typical teenager in most other aspects of my life, talking with my best friend about how scared I was to be kissed for the first time, and how scared I was to *not* be kissed for the first time. I worried aloud about tests and homework and boys and girls and clothes, but I kept the dark stuff hidden where I thought it belonged—deep inside me until I could manage my own way out of the abyss. Years passed and obsessions intensified. The nature of the obsessions changed, but they never really went away. There were obsessive peaks and valleys, good days and bad days, even good months and bad months.

By the time I was 26 years old I was utterly exhausted. I had been fighting a particular type of obsession—my fear that I would harm a child—off and on for about five years. It intensified when I was in serious relationships, because marriage and family felt like logical next steps. That fear remained in tucked-away corners of my brain even when I was single. It was becoming as stubborn as I was—it wasn't willing to leave, and I wasn't planning to tell anyone what was going on.

A mental showdown.

I won that showdown. But not before I hit rock bottom, a few months after I met and started dating the man who would become my husband. So I guess you could say I fell from cloud nine and slammed into rock bottom, an even more devastating experience than I could ever have anticipated.

Peter and I hit it off immediately, and we were soon spending as much time together as possible.

Our relationship quickly grew serious, which was exhilarating and frightening at the same time. You know the old nursery rhyme: First comes love, then comes marriage, then comes the baby in the baby carriage.

Love? Check. Marriage? Quite possibly. Baby? No way. The deeper I fell in love, the worse I felt about my life. What if Peter wanted kids? I told him how I felt, leaving out details about my obsessions: *I don't want kids, not now, and probably not ever.* Once he convinced me he was okay with that and being with me didn't mean he was giving up on any dreams of fatherhood, I felt a huge sense of relief.

The relief was short-lived. I had thought that if we could establish once and for all that I didn't have to raise children I would be better. But that's not how you overcome an obsession—avoiding it is just a less obvious type of compulsion. Rather than facing it head-on, I was trying to run in the other direction.

So it should come as no surprise that not only did I not get better, I got worse. I could decide not to create my own children who I would have to live with day in and day out, but kids still exist in the world. I began to fear I could hurt any child in my care, my future nieces and nephews and my friends' children—or even random children.

It became excruciatingly painful to be around children at all. I didn't even want to go to a mall or grocery store because I knew there would be children there. I would immediately panic upon seeing a child, even one who was with a parent, because all I could do was obsess.

At night I would try to keep my eyes open until my eyelids were so heavy that I would fall asleep without ever having to be awake with my eyes closed. If I were awake beneath my lids there was no telling what images I would be bombarded with. If lying in bed didn't go well, I'd move to the couch and fall asleep in front of the TV. That way I never felt like it was just me and my thoughts. One night, though, I woke up to the words "Kids are everywhere." It was a commercial for a household cleaner that was safe to use everywhere, even on high-chair trays, but I felt taunted. It was just what I didn't want to hear: You can try to escape all you want, but kids are everywhere. What are you gonna do, refuse to leave your apartment? It was my personal hell's version of "You can run, but you cannot hide."

I felt so alone. I had friends and family and especially my boyfriend to lean on, but if I couldn't reveal the real reason for my depression, how could I ever really feel comforted? To say I was depressed is an understatement. Not only could I not have kids because I was afraid I'd cause them irreparable harm, but I couldn't function normally any longer because the thoughts were so horrible.

I had felt this miserable in years past, but I had always pulled through it well enough to go on living a fairly normal life. This time it became abundantly clear that I needed professional help, but it took me a while to reach this realization, and I tried to carry on with regular activities like going to the gym, going to work, and seeing friends.

One thing that had made me feel better from time to time was the small hope that it would all go away eventually, that things couldn't continue to get worse, or even stay the same. The trouble is that life most certainly can get worse, and the old adage "Whatever doesn't kill you makes you stronger" is laughable. Each time I emerged from a depressive period, I was weaker, more beaten down, wearier, and more afraid.

During the few months I struggled with these obsessive thoughts, there were several hopeful moments when I thought I might finally be okay. Unfortunately, those moments were just that—brief snippets of time when my old self pushed itself to the surface and let me breathe. I was happiest when I was with Peter, but being with him felt unbearable nonetheless. I was able to cry up until he came over to visit; after that I would hold it in and try to be myself. Sometimes hugging him and cuddling with him made me feel better because I loved him so much and I felt how much he loved me, but more often than not it made me feel worse because I wanted our relationship to be so much more. I didn't want to just be happy enough to stave off soft sobs; I wanted to be truly happy, and I wanted Peter to be happy.

Many of my crying spells began because of the guilt I felt in dating him. I felt I was being utterly selfish; he didn't deserve to be with a crazy person, I told myself, and I considered breaking it off. The idea of letting him go was unbelievably painful, even though it held some possibility of relief. At least I could fully focus on my health if I didn't have to worry about how my problems were affecting him. But when I imagined our breakup scenario, I didn't see myself telling him the whole truth, so he would be left to wonder why I was ending things. If I told him I was depressed and didn't want him to be subjected to that, I knew he would insist on staying with me and helping me through it. I also believed that if I told him what was depressing me—my obsessive thoughts—he would be horrified and would never want to see me again. I couldn't stand the thought of him hating me, so I continued to keep it secret, all the while knowing he deserved to know everything about me if he were going to be with me forever.

One night Peter, a musician, had a gig at a boathouse and wanted me to watch him play. I worked on the book I was proofreading until I couldn't sit alone on my couch any longer, and then I went to the show.

The drive felt long. Day had already given in to night, and I became hopelessly lost. I maneuvered my car along twisty, construction-filled roads, listening to an old mixtape a friend had made me in college. The songs spoke to my mood with their heartbreaking lyrics and melancholy tone. Elliott Smith's soothing voice came across the crackling speakers like an old friend as he sang a particularly moving song I had identified with during another obsessive period in college. But even though his words made me feel less alone, they also reminded me of just how depressed I was. I felt that Elliott was directing everything toward me as he slowly crooned heartbreaking lyrics about images that get stuck in the head and won't go away no matter how much you try to push them out.

I felt better knowing there was someone out there who seemed to understand, but then I remembered the cold, hard truth—that this man, the one person who seemed to get me without ever having met me, had eventually killed himself. Not only that, hearing the lyrics "images stuck in your head" reminded me of my own persistent and ugly images. I turned off the music with a shaky index finger and continued to drive in silence. I briefly considered swerving off the road, but I was pretty sure doing so would only injure me and perhaps someone else. I didn't think I would ever be able to find Peter, but I was willing to try because going home alone was not an option. I needed to see him, to be among people.

I felt better when I finally reached my destination, but of course the change of pace wasn't enough to make me forget all of my worries. Before Peter's band went on stage, a band made up of family members, including a teenage boy, played. The boy was quite impressive, and his grandparents and other relatives watched him with joy and pride and hugged him afterward. Seeing this made me think again that I would never be normal, because these people effortlessly showed physical affection to a kid. They obviously weren't paralyzed by terrifying thoughts of harming him.

Later in our relationship, Peter and I went to lunch one day, and a bunch of kids were running around the restaurant. I said something to the effect of, "If I were a parent I'd be too worried to let my kids out of my sight," and then said, "but I'm not, and I won't be, thank God."

Peter frowned. "The only thing that bothers me . . ." He hesitated before going on, and when he did he sounded pained. "If you don't want kids, that's okay. I'm fine with that. But what bothers me is that you think you might not be a good mom."

"I know, I know I would be," I said as reassuringly as I could, but I wasn't convinced. I tried to brush it off, but we had both gotten a little choked up.

Finally, I was hurting enough that I reached out, just a little, for help. It was Peter's birthday and we were on our way to a bowling alley to meet a bunch of his friends. I had tried hard to make his day special even though he had to work late into the evening, presenting him with a cake from our neighborhood bakery in addition to a gift. I also put on a happy face, trying to mask what I was feeling inside—a mixture of total despair and numbness. I felt guilty. I wished for at least this one day that I could actually be happy. I wanted to be peppy so I could really help him celebrate rather than just being along for the ride. Instead, I was dead weight.

"I'm sorry that I haven't been happy lately," I said.

"Oh, baby, it's okay. I love you," Peter reassured me.

"I . . . I wonder if I need to go on medication. People think I'm happy all the time, but I'm not." A friend had nicknamed me "Ali Sunshine" in college; she even made me a key chain with an *A, L,* and *I* on each block and a yellow smiley-face sun bookending my name. When I was in a relationship with a guy who was depressed much of the time, my oldest friend thought we were mismatched: "You aren't like that," she said. "You're a happy person."

I liked that I was able to be nice to people and that they felt that I had a warm personality, but I often became frustrated when people refused to acknowledge that I was indeed sad sometimes, too. My bright exterior was a cover-up of the darkness I often felt inside.

"You aren't suicidal, are you?" Peter asked.

"No," I said, hoping my tone was convincing. I actually had considered suicide, but I wasn't sure if I could call myself "suicidal." How serious did one have to be in order to be classified as suicidal? The truth was that I had become so distraught that there were moments when I truly felt death was the only escape, but I wasn't so far gone that I considered it a real option, and it wasn't at all desirable. I *did* want to live, but only if my life didn't have to continue as it had been going.

Important Note: OCD can cause depression, which can lead to thoughts of suicide. If you're thinking about suicide, please talk to an adult you trust right away. You can also call the National Suicide Prevention Lifeline (1-800-273-8255) or go to their website for a live chat (suicidepreventionlifeline.org). A skilled, trained counselor will be there to help you 24/7.

WHAT IS OCD?

I know now that what I was going through is called obsessive-compulsive disorder, an illness that, as I noted earlier, affects about 1 in 100 adults and 1 in 200 kids, and usually strikes between the ages of 8 and 12 or the late teens and early adulthood.

Mental health professionals refer to the *Diagnostic and Statistical Manual of Mental Disorders (DSM),* the bible of mental health diagnoses, to determine whether a patient has OCD. According to the most recent edition of the *DSM (DSM-5),* a person with OCD is plagued by *obsessions*—recurrent, persistent, and distressing thoughts, impulses, or images—and *compulsions*—repetitive behaviors or mental acts the person performs in response to the obsessions. Engaging in the compulsive behavior usually stops the obsessions, but only temporarily. And unfortunately, this temporary relief reinforces the compulsive behavior because it seems to work.

An "OCD brain" actually looks different from the brain of a person who doesn't have OCD. (Google "OCD brain scan" to see side-by-side images of different brains.) The brain of a person with OCD will look especially different in certain cortical and subcortical regions and will appear to be a hotbed of activity of rapidly firing neurons. Some scientists believe that too much activity in certain parts of the brain keeps obsessive thoughts from turning off. It's pretty fascinating—and validating—to see a visual picture of our disorder.

While everyone has obsessive-compulsive tendencies every once in a while, if you've been diagnosed with OCD it's because your obsessions and compulsions have taken over your life, interrupting and prolonging your daily activities, making routines take longer than they should, and taking the joy out of your favorite pastimes.

Prior to a formal diagnosis, you may be asked to fill out a checklist like the one that follows (I completed a similar checklist of obsessions and compulsions before my first appointment with my psychiatrist). See how many obsessions and compulsions you relate to, and consider how much they are affecting your daily life.

COMMON OBSESSIONS IN OCD*

Contamination

☐ Body fluids (examples: urine, feces)

☐ Germs/disease (examples: herpes, HIV)

☐ Environmental contaminants (examples: asbestos, radiation)

☐ Household chemicals (examples: cleaners, solvents)

☐ Dirt

Losing Control

☐ Fear of acting on an impulse to harm oneself

☐ Fear of acting on an impulse to harm others

☐ Fear of violent or horrific images in one's mind

☐ Fear of blurting out obscenities or insults

☐ Fear of stealing things

Harm

☐ Fear of being responsible for something terrible happening (examples: fire, burglary)

☐ Fear of harming others because of not being careful enough (example: dropping something on the ground that might cause someone to slip and hurt him/herself)

Obsessions Related to Perfectionism

☐ Concern about evenness or exactness

☐ Concern with a need to know or remember

☐ Fear of losing or forgetting important information when throwing something out

☐ Inability to decide whether to keep or to discard things

☐ Fear of losing things

Unwanted Sexual Thoughts

☐ Forbidden or perverse sexual thoughts or images

☐ Forbidden or perverse sexual impulses about others

☐ Obsessions about homosexuality

---

*Reprinted with permission of New Harbinger Publications, Inc. This is an adaptation of the OC Checklist which appears in S. Wilhelm and G. S. Steketee's *Cognitive Therapy for Obsessive-Compulsive Disorder: A Guide for Professionals* (2006), www.newharbinger.com.

☐ Sexual obsessions that involve children or incest

☐ Obsessions about aggressive sexual behavior toward others

Religious Obsessions (Scrupulosity)

☐ Concern with offending God, or concern about blasphemy

☐ Excessive concern with right/wrong or morality

Other Obsessions

☐ Concern with getting a physical illness or disease (not by contamination; example: cancer)

☐ Superstitious ideas about lucky/unlucky numbers, certain colors

COMMON COMPULSIONS IN OCD

Washing and Cleaning

☐ Washing hands excessively or in a certain way

☐ Excessive showering, bathing, tooth brushing, grooming, or toilet routines

☐ Cleaning household items or other objects excessively

☐ Doing other things to prevent or remove contact with contaminants

Checking

☐ Checking that you did not/will not harm others

☐ Checking that you did not/will not harm yourself

☐ Checking that nothing terrible happened

☐ Checking that you did not make a mistake

☐ Checking some parts of your physical condition or body

Repeating

☐ Rereading or rewriting

☐ Repeating routine activities (examples: going in or out doors, getting up or down from chairs)

☐ Repeating body movements (examples: tapping, touching, blinking)

☐ Repeating activities in "multiples" (examples: doing a task three times because three is a "good," "right," or "safe" number)

Mental Compulsions

☐ Mental review of events to prevent harm (to oneself, to others; to prevent terrible consequences)

☐ Praying to prevent harm (to oneself or others; to prevent terrible consequences)

☐ Counting while performing a task to end on a "good," "right," or "safe" number

☐ "Canceling" or "undoing" (example: replacing a "bad" word with a "good" word to cancel it out)

Other Compulsions

☐ Collecting items, which results in significant clutter in the home (also called hoarding)*

☐ Putting things in order or arranging things until it "feels right"

☐ Telling, asking, or confessing to get reassurance

☐ Avoiding situations that might trigger your obsessions

How many did you check off? One? Two? Fifteen?

You don't have to check off every last item on the list in order to be diagnosed with OCD. It's not how many obsessions you have, it's the intensity of the one or two you do have and how having them affects your day-to-day life.

IT'S OFFICIAL: I HAVE OCD

Since you're reading this book, you probably checked off some items from the list. Here is how my own list looks if I include all my symptoms from over the years.

COMMON OBSESSIONS IN OCD

Contamination

☐ Body fluids (examples: urine, feces)

☐ Germs/disease (examples: herpes, HIV)

☐ Environmental contaminants (examples: asbestos, radiation)

☐ Household chemicals (examples: cleaners, solvents)

☐ Dirt

---

*In the most current *Diagnostic Statistical Manual*, the *DSM-5*, hoarding is no longer included as a symptom of OCD. It is now classified as a separate disorder and is listed under its own entry; however, the International OCD Foundation still addresses hoarding as a symptom of OCD.

Losing Control

☑ Fear of acting on an impulse to harm oneself

☑ Fear of acting on an impulse to harm others

☑ Fear of violent or horrific images in one's mind

☑ Fear of blurting out obscenities or insults

☐ Fear of stealing things

Harm

☑ Fear of being responsible for something terrible happening (examples: fire, burglary)

☑ Fear of harming others because of not being careful enough (example: dropping something on the ground that might cause someone to slip and hurt him/herself)

Obsessions Related to Perfectionism

☑ Concern about evenness or exactness

☑ Concern with a need to know or remember

☐ Fear of losing or forgetting important information when throwing something out

☑ Inability to decide whether to keep or to discard things

☐ Fear of losing things

Unwanted Sexual Thoughts

☑ Forbidden or perverse sexual thoughts or images

☑ Forbidden or perverse sexual impulses about others

☑ Obsessions about homosexuality

☑ Sexual obsessions that involve children or incest

☑ Obsessions about aggressive sexual behavior toward others

Religious Obsessions (Scrupulosity)

☑ Concern with offending God, or concern about blasphemy

☑ Excessive concern with right/wrong or morality

Other Obsessions

☑ Concern with getting a physical illness or disease (not by contamination; example: cancer)

☐ Superstitious ideas about lucky/unlucky numbers, certain colors

COMMON COMPULSIONS IN OCD

Washing and Cleaning

☐ Washing hands excessively or in a certain way

☑ Excessive showering, bathing, tooth brushing, grooming, or toilet routines

☐ Cleaning household items or other objects excessively

☐ Doing other things to prevent or remove contact with contaminants

Checking

☐ Checking that you did not/will not harm others

☐ Checking that you did not/will not harm yourself

☐ Checking that nothing terrible happened

☑ Checking that you did not make a mistake

☑ Checking some parts of your physical condition or body

Repeating

☑ Rereading or rewriting

☐ Repeating routine activities (examples: going in or out doors, getting up or down from chairs)

☑ Repeating body movements (examples: tapping, touching, blinking)

☐ Repeating activities in "multiples" (examples: doing a task three times because three is a "good," "right," or "safe" number)

Mental Compulsions

☑ Mental review of events to prevent harm (to oneself, to others; to prevent terrible consequences)

☑ Praying to prevent harm (to oneself or others; to prevent terrible consequences)

☑ Counting while performing a task to end on a "good," "right," or "safe" number

☐ "Canceling" or "undoing" (example: replacing a "bad" word with a "good" word to cancel it out)

Other Compulsions

☐ Collecting items, which results in significant clutter in the home (also called hoarding)

☐ Putting things in order or arranging things until it "feels right"

☑ Telling, asking, or confessing to get reassurance

☑ Avoiding situations that might trigger your obsessions

WHAT DO OCD SYMPTOMS LOOK LIKE?

I checked off many symptoms on the list, and I'll try to explain some of them here so you get a better idea of how OCD can manifest itself. Maybe you'll even relate to something I've shared.

☑ Counting while performing a task to end on a "good," "right," or "safe" number

☑ Repeating body movements (examples: tapping, touching, blinking)

I have always had an annoying habit of counting each syllable of conversations, my thoughts, dialogue on TV, and song lyrics on each corner of my feet. I start with my big toe on my left foot and count in a figure eight. The perfect ending is on the right side of my right heel. Eight syllables is ideal. Or sixteen. Or twenty-four. You get the point.

If someone is talking to me and says something such as, "The elephant is sad today," all is right in my little counting world. If the person instead says, "The elephant was sad yesterday," I try to keep the conversation going so the last syllable doesn't end on the beginning of the counting cycle instead of the end. When I've counted nine syllables on my feet, I feel an uneven weight on the big toe of my left foot. It feels heavier, and I feel an urge to respond to "The elephant was sad yesterday" with "Was it? That's really too bad."

If I am watching TV and the commercial's last syllable ends on an "odd" number on my feet, I try to fill in the rest with the appropriate number of syllables in my thoughts—but this usually doesn't satisfy me, because making up thoughts so I can land on an even number leaves me with uneven weight on those corners of my feet. My big toe on my left foot, for example, will seem heavy and dark, and the rest of my toes, the ones filled with my rushed thoughts, will feel light, almost as though no words have entered my mind at all. Spoken or heard syllables carry more weight and importance in my feet than my own thoughts, but if I am reading silently to myself, the syllables carry a weight that is equal to oral syllables. It is only when I try to force things to be perfect and to fall into place that the whole process goes awry.

☑ Concern with getting a physical illness or disease (not by contamination; example: cancer)

As a kid, I always believed I was going to be affected with whatever a character in a book or movie had.

☑ Excessive showering, bathing, tooth brushing, grooming, or toilet routines

While I've never had a germ obsession, I did go through a period of really long showers and washing my clothes every time I wore them for even a short amount of time, even my sweaters and jeans, which drove my mom crazy. She kept telling me I could wear them more than once without washing them, especially if I was wearing a shirt under the sweater, but I wouldn't listen.

I guess you could say I was a typical teenager in how much time I spent in the bathroom, but no one else seemed to understand why I took such long showers, and I had a hard time explaining it. First I had to stand under the water and get completely wet, and then I had to make sure my entire washcloth was evenly wet, with no dry spots at all, and then I would scrub my face with it, wash my face with soap, wipe the soap off with the washcloth, and finally make sure I rinsed all of the soap suds off the washcloth. I think this is what took the most time—the standing in the shower doing nothing but rinsing my washcloth, turning it over and over in my hands, not satisfied until it was suds-free.

☑ Obsessions about homosexuality

When I was in middle school, I was afraid I was gay. I was young, Christian, and very into church. I hadn't even dated a boy yet, but I had been convinced by some religious reading materials and church members that being homosexual was wrong, so of course that's what

I obsessed about. It turned into an uncontrollable obsession; I would cry and pray and test myself by watching TV shows with beautiful women to see what I thought or felt. I remember watching *Beverly Hills 90210* in eighth grade with a friend. The character Brenda was lying on the beach with her boyfriend, Dylan, and I asked myself over and over again if I thought she was pretty. Did I find her attractive? Did I want to stare at Brenda more than at Dylan?

This obsession came and went through high school. I think I was finally able to let it go when I believed in my own principles more than my church's. After all, *I* didn't think being gay was wrong—if it turned out I was, who cares? And, ultimately, I wasn't. Deep down I was always interested in boys.

☑ Concern with offending God, or concern about blasphemy

☑ Excessive concern with right/wrong or morality

☑ Praying to prevent harm (to oneself or others; to prevent terrible consequences)

Toward the end of high school, I began to have serious doubts about Christianity. I tearfully asked God why those who have never been taught about Jesus should go to hell because they don't believe in him, or why people who *do* know about Jesus but aren't Christian should be punished. These normal questions became ugly obsessive thoughts, bringing me into one of the worst depressive periods I had ever had, coming and going throughout my four years at a Lutheran college. I would sob by myself in my dorm room and offer desperate prayers to the God I thought I was constantly betraying, but I didn't think I was depressed. I thought depressed people must feel much worse than I did (I'm not sure how), so I didn't feel worthy of identifying myself as such. My religious obsessions plagued me for four years, before I moved on to my next greatest fear: being a bad mother.

☑ Fear of acting on an impulse to harm others

☑ Forbidden or perverse sexual thoughts or images

☑ Forbidden or perverse sexual impulses about others

☑ Sexual obsessions that involve children or incest

☑ Avoiding situations that might trigger your obsessions

Out of all the checkmarks I put on that list, these obsessions were the hardest to conquer. As intense as my other obsessions had felt, these plunged me into the worst depression. My greatest fear stemmed from what was once my greatest dream. I had babysat the girls next door to my family all through high school. When I was at their house on a Saturday night I loved to imagine my life with a husband and children. I couldn't wait to be done with adolescence so I could finally begin the life I had always wanted. All that mattered to me was that I'd one day be a mother, that I'd get to hold a baby in my arms and nurture it the way only a parent can. At that point in my life, I was even excited about my kids growing up, because I imagined they'd always be babies to me—sweet, precious, brilliant, and funny.

It wasn't until I was in a serious post-college relationship that the fear of harming my own children seeped into my psyche. Motherhood didn't seem like a far-off dream anymore. It seemed like a real possibility, and my brain couldn't handle it. All it took was one terrible image to pop into my brain, and I was doomed to years of harm obsessions.

I think the reason this theme of obsessions was so unrelenting was that following through with any of them really would be bad. I was eventually able to stop obsessing about the possibility of being gay when I realized that being gay is not in and of itself bad. And plenty of people have religious doubts and even outright, unapologetic disbelief in a higher power, so ultimately I was still a decent person even if I had "bad" religious thoughts.

But obsessing about hurting someone so vulnerable was different. I couldn't just brush it off and say, "So what if I *did* abuse a kid? That'd be okay!" Um, no, it would not. That was possibly the worst part of this latest obsession. I had to come up with a whole different way of coping, and until I sought outside help I was ill equipped to do so.

When I did finally see a doctor, he shook his head when I told him I didn't think I'd be able to get over this obsession because it was so awful. I had a hard time believing him when he said I'd be able to get past it as I had the others—but not because I'd be able to write it off as no big deal. He knew it was a big deal, to say the least, and yet he knew he'd be able to help me get through it in a totally different way than I'd gotten through things before. He was going to equip me with the proper tools.

And that was important. I learned that although I was able to get over those other obsessions once I stopped perceiving them as bad, this wasn't the right way to go about it. Until I was addressing the root of my problem, I would always obsess about *something*. Without coping methods, the obsessions will always get out of control. Dismissing the topic itself wasn't enough. So you might disagree with me very strongly that it's okay to question God, or even that there's nothing wrong with homosexuality, and that's okay—because thinking the subject of your obsession is "okay" isn't a legitimate coping method. That solution is more like using one of those small adhesive bandages on a gaping wound when what's needed is stitches and antibiotics.

TYPES OF OCD

Having OCD means different things to different people, as evidenced by the detailed checklist you read earlier on pages 15–17. Some researchers say there are two main types of obsessions, called *autogenous* and *reactive*. Autogenous obsessions are the type I have struggled with: involuntary, shameful thoughts that seem to come out of nowhere. Reactive obsessions are caused by external events and include fears about contamination, accidents, or a need for perfection.

If you spend any time researching OCD, you'll find different categories with different names and descriptions. For example, one article I read listed five types of OCD, another four, and yet another nine: washing, cleaning, checking, repeating, "hit and run," orderliness, need for symmetry, sexual obsessions, and fear of loss of impulse control. Whew! But I find the checklist I've included here to be the most helpful in understanding what constitutes obsessions and compulsions, because it is so exhaustive—it includes just about every category you could imagine.

Hoarding has long been considered a type of OCD, but in the *DSM-5,* the most recent volume, it is now in its own distinct category. While these changes and different ideas about what OCD is and isn't can be confusing, I find it comforting to know that researchers continue to seek answers and to learn more about what people like you and I struggle with.

Here are descriptions of some identified and common types of OCD.

Religious, Violent, and Sexual (Taboo) Obsessions

Whatever you consider the worst and oddest taboo obsession you've ever had, someone else—maybe me—has had something very similar or even the same. A book that really helped me with my taboo obsessions, *The Imp of the Mind: Exploring the Silent Epidemic of Obsessive Bad Thoughts* by Lee Baer, Ph.D., has lots of real-life examples. Here are a few:

- A priest can't stop staring at women's breasts when he walks down the street.
- A young man fears wanting to have sex with animals.
- A woman fears wanting to have sex with her young son.
- A man fears he will become a mass murderer.
- A man fears he will yell racist slurs at people in public.
- A young man fears he will harm his parents and his girlfriend.
- A woman believes she will spend eternity in hell.

Even Martin Luther, a German monk, priest, professor of theology, and the father of Lutheranism, feared he would curse God and Jesus and had images of "the Devil's behind" while praying.

You might have religious obsessions if you pray all the time, constantly pray on the rosary, or go to church or confession more than usual, especially if you are engaging in these practices out of fear and not because they bring you joy or make you feel closer to God in a positive way. If you are fearful that God will punish you over bad thoughts, this is most likely an obsession and not a common worry or drive to be devout.

Or maybe you have sexual or violent obsessions, which can be quite painful because you associate the behaviors you obsess about with "bad" people—you don't see yourself as the kind of person who would do bad things, but the fear that you might is upsetting and overwhelming. And, in fact, that association is exactly why people with OCD are *not* likely to follow through on these obsessions. If thoughts like these become obsessions for you, it is probably because you already know they're wrong and because you are devoted to being the best person possible.

With these obsessions, not only are you afraid you will harm someone or do something illegal or blasphemous, you also feel so guilty that you are thinking these thoughts at all that you may become depressed. It doesn't help you to know that the thoughts are not desired or that they make you feel ill, you still feel bad that you have them.

Before I was diagnosed with OCD and found help, there were several times I became depressed and even considered suicide.* I couldn't understand where the obsessions came from and why I couldn't just turn them off. They were so unwelcome!

One night, utterly frustrated and worn down by the relentless images, I stood in front of my bathroom mirror, crying, and stared at my face. I looked like myself—sweet, innocent, normal—so I couldn't understand why my mind was torturing me. It was as though my mind had been taken hostage by someone immoral and dirty, someone who was forcing me to think unbearable thoughts.

These thoughts did not feel like my own because they would come to me out of the blue and hit me with such intensity that at times they took my breath away. They always made my stomach twist with nausea, made me break into a panicked sweat. What was compelling me to think the unthinkable, and *why couldn't I stop it?* The more I tried to stop the thoughts, repetitive words, and bombardment of terrifying images, the worse everything became.

If you're like me and have OCD that revolves around bad thoughts, you probably obsess about whatever you find the most morally reprehensible. That is what OCD does: It takes a fear or thought society already considers bad (murder, incest, racism) and magnifies it. What if someone standing in front of you said, "Whatever you do, don't picture me naked!" Would you have a hard time *not* picturing the person naked—even if you really, really didn't want to? (Hello, Great-Aunt Norma!)

Thoughts are just thoughts—they don't mean you'll act on them, and having bad thoughts doesn't make you a bad person. It's just hard convincing your "OCD brain"!

---

*If you're thinking about suicide, please talk to a trusted adult right away or contact the National Suicide Prevention Lifeline (see page 13).

Checking/Obsessions About Harm

Some people with OCD obsess about the possibility that something horrible will happen because of something they've done or not done. Maybe you're afraid that if you think a not-so-nice thought about someone harm will come to them, or if you don't check the stove to make sure it's turned off a fire will break out.

A person with "checking" OCD might look several times—and maybe a specific but seemingly arbitrary number of times—to make sure the stove is turned off. Another may continue to drive around her block until she feels sure that she didn't run over a child who was crossing the street. (See Sophie's story on page 30 about her fear that harm will come to people listed in her phone contacts.)

Karissa's Story: What If?

As I walked up the stairs, I watched my right foot touch the crack. If it didn't touch it, I went back and started over. Whenever I put clothes on, I checked the size to make sure each garment was mine even if I knew it was. After I washed my hands, I would smell them to make sure they smelled clean. If they didn't, I would go back in the bathroom to rewash my hands.

Homework took forever. I sat there for hours struggling while I read and reread the paragraphs. I checked my counting in math over and over again. I could have missed something. I went through what homework I did and what I still needed to do over and over again. What if I missed something? What if? That was a big fear of mine. Another was the longing for satisfaction that OCD needed. Doing my homework, I needed to get everything perfect. When I was writing, if it did not look perfectly neat, I would erase and erase again until OCD was satisfied. I would start homework right after school, eat, and go back to homework until 10:30 at night with no break. My parents helped as much as possible. My parents and teachers worked out a plan which included a certain amount of time to spend on each subject. It was difficult for me though because I wanted my homework to be perfect and finished.

The movie *Freaky Friday* became a nightmare. After I watched that, I worried about switching places with people. If I simply even touched somebody, I had to touch them again because I thought I might switch places with them in the morning. My life would not be the same. Sometimes, OCD would make me think that if I did not do something before I went to sleep, in the morning the world would not be the same. This scared me into thinking that the world would be different because of me, and I would not know how to change it.

Karissa was 13 years old when she wrote this essay. Since then she has gone through intensive residential treatment and is doing much better. On leaving treatment she wrote, "I plan to continue with my motivation to take control of OCD instead of letting OCD control me."

You might know that it's not logical to believe that your thoughts or actions have a direct impact on the well-being of others, but you care so much and are so concerned that you can't help but perform the compulsions in an attempt to prevent anything bad from happening. Exposure and response prevention therapy has helped people just like you stop performing compulsions (see page 60). Eventually you will see that *not* performing the compulsions doesn't cause harm and you won't be burdened by them anymore.

Germ Phobias and Cleaning Rituals

Cleaning compulsions, particularly hand-washing rituals, are perhaps the most recognizable OCD symptoms. It's a common misconception that excessive washing is the *only* symptom of OCD, and this may be because it's the easiest to depict on TV and in movies. But that doesn't mean it's well understood.

While some cleaning rituals do stem from a germ phobia, sometimes a person excessively washes herself or her surrounding environment in an attempt to ward off "magical" contamination as well. For example, a person may fear becoming ill or being seriously injured simply by hearing the name of an illness or seeing a picture of a disabled person.

A person with contamination-related obsessions doesn't take a once-daily 10-minute shower—he will repeatedly wash his hands, shower, or disinfect himself or his possessions and will never feel clean enough. He may also avoid whatever he believes will make him sick, such as other people or the outside world in general. Avoiding fears is a compulsive behavior as well.

Josh's Story: I Had a Germ Phobia

My OCD, much like many others', started off as what you might call a series of quirks. In my freshman year of high school, my inner circle found themselves both confused and amused by the copious amount of soap I used whenever I washed my hands. I convinced myself that I was simply being thorough and thought no more of it. But little by little, it got worse. The progression was so incremental that I didn't even notice until it was too late. By the time my senior year rolled around, I viewed my school, and everything within it, as a microbial minefield, and the mere thought of bringing those filthy, disgusting books home and into my personal space made me physically ill.

Josh was 24 when he wrote this.

WHY DO I HAVE OCD?

At my most depressed I'd ask this question. Had I done something wrong? Was I being punished for things I had done or hadn't done, thought or hadn't thought?

No one knows exactly why some people have OCD, but I now know I wasn't being "punished" and my obsessions weren't because I did something wrong. The reason for OCD may be different for each individual. For one person it might be how the immune system responded to a bout of strep throat; for another it might be genetics. There are several possible reasons behind OCD.

Traumatic Events, Stress Triggers, and Life Changes

While everyday stress alone doesn't cause OCD, life changes—both positive and negative—can trigger symptoms. These life events could include the death of a loved one, the birth of a sibling, a parent's divorce or remarriage, starting at a new school, moving to a new home or community, or enduring a natural disaster.

I had several life changes before my OCD symptoms became unbearable. I had moved into an apartment by myself, started a new job that stressed me out, and begun a serious relationship with Peter—undoubtedly a happy turn of events but disruptive to my normal routine nonetheless.

Then I was in a minor car accident right before my obsessions became truly unbearable. I wasn't seriously hurt, but my car was totaled, meaning I had to quickly find a replacement, and a new car payment wasn't in my budget. On top of that, I was so busy at work I couldn't take any time off, so I had to squeeze in insurance phone calls and searches for used cars I could actually afford. I was beyond busy, all while trying to stop obsessing.

Without time to take the occasional deep breath and calm myself down, my obsessions came on with a new intensity. I had read somewhere that a traumatic event can cause OCD, but since the car accident wasn't on par with being abused or witnessing a murder, I figured it couldn't be the culprit. Desperate for answers, I tried to remember anything I might have forgotten. Did something happen in my childhood that was so terrible that my brain made me repress it? These doubts led to nothing but trouble, and even more obsessions.

Sophie's Story, Part 1: My OCD Started with a Dog Attack

My mum and dad had a New Year's Eve party every year. One year, something crazy happened. One of my neighbors kicked open our front door, chucked his three dogs into the house, and told them to kill. Our house was full of people and children, and the three dogs started to chase everybody. They managed to attack my dad and my dog before my dad and brother got control of them and got them out of the house. Although we had to bring my dog to the vet, no one was seriously injured—but the experience was terrifying.

After that night, I would check to make sure all the windows and doors were locked every 10 minutes, and if I wasn't checking them I was asking my parents if they were closed and locked. These issues soon escalated into other things, such as going around my house turning off the light switches, and repeating these over and over again—on, off, on, off—shouting down the stairs to my parents to come and check. I was unable to settle down to sleep with these worries going through my mind. Things got so bad, I inadvertently defrosted my parents' freezer by turning off the plug. My parents would often oversleep because I would sneak into their bedroom during the night and unplug their alarm clock.

It wasn't long before I got another obsession with running faucets, ovens, and stove burners. Soon my parents realized there was a serious problem, and they then took me to a doctor who referred me to a child psychologist who helped me learn how to deal with my demons. After a period of time he discharged me. I am now 17 years of age, and 90 percent of the issues I described are no longer with me.

Sophie was 17 when she wrote this essay. To read more of her story, go to Part 2 on page 33.

Genetics

My mom's side of the family has a running joke that we have something called the Gunderson gene, which explains why we tend to worry so much. Since I can trace anxiety back a few generations, I think genetics has played a role in my OCD symptoms.

Maybe you have your dad's eyes, your mom's nose, and your grandma's brain—not literally, of course. If you're a lot like one of your older relatives, maybe it's because you both have a dysfunction in the neuronal loop that runs from your orbital frontal cortex to the cingulate gyrus, striatum (caudate nucleus and putamen), globus pallidus, and thalamus, and back to the frontal cortex.

Huh? In plain English: Maybe the front part of your brain has a hard time communicating with the deeper parts of your brain. Or maybe certain parts of your brain are overactive, which might explain why you can't just turn off your thoughts and think of something else.

Studies of identical twins have shown that if one sibling has OCD, the other is more likely to have it as well; other family studies show that having a blood relative with OCD increases the likelihood that you will have OCD, too.

Strep Throat

Although the connection between strep throat and OCD is still being researched, sometimes children develop PANDAS (pediatric autoimmune neuropsychiatric disorders associated with streptococcal infections). In other words, they get OCD after they have strep throat. But it's not because of the strep throat itself. Rather, a person's immune system develops antibodies to fight the bacteria, and it's these antibodies that somehow result in OCD.

When I first heard this, I felt like a light bulb flashed on above my head and everything clicked. I racked my brain, rummaging through childhood memories. Had I ever had strep throat? When? But as I thought about it, I wasn't sure. I had been tested for it many times when I had sore throats that lingered for too many days; I have clear memories of instinctively grabbing at the doctor's arms because he was gagging me with the long cotton swab, but I couldn't remember if any of the results ever came back positive.

So I emailed my mom and asked her if I had ever had strep throat, and her response was that she couldn't remember for sure, but she said she thought so because they "don't just give antibiotics for no reason." I guess that means I was prescribed antibiotics at one time or another, and I guess they were the type prescribed for strep throat. But without clearer evidence or a better memory, I can't say that strep throat resulted in my OCD symptoms.

WHAT NOW?

If you're like me, you probably want to learn all you can about OCD and its possible causes. This book will never be able to cover all of the amazing scientific research behind OCD, but there are countless reading materials out there.

The bigger question might be whether it *matters* why I have OCD, or why any of us have it, or if all that matters is where we go from the point of diagnosis. I think it is important to increase awareness so family adults know what to look for in case their children have OCD, but as far as you and I are concerned, looking back and trying to figure out the *whys* instead of the *what nows* could just serve to add to our anxiety and make us feel worse.

Sophie's Story, Part 2: I Got the Help I Needed

My earlier obsessions are no longer with me, but they have been replaced with other issues such as a lack of confidence and feeling negative all of the time. I don't go out of my house and I don't like to leave my parents.

Eventually my OCD symptoms concerned myself more than my house. My mobile phone began to drive me insane; I would constantly check to make sure no one's name was listed on my contacts page because I was afraid something bad would happen to that person. Even though it was painful, I would press really hard into my eyes to try to get the bad visions out of my head.

After waiting for another referral to see somebody about my OCD, I finally got an appointment with a new therapist. When I got there the man was very polite and helped me through a lot. He spoke to me with my mum and dad there, too, but he also needed to see me alone and asked me questions that had to do with my OCD. I was in the room about one hour and he told me that he was going to put me under the care of a different therapist and that it would take another five or six weeks before I could get in.

It was hard to wait, but my new therapist and I are working together to beat my demons. The therapist told me it doesn't mean someone's going to die if my contact page shows his or her name, and I actually listened to what he said. I haven't checked my phone as much as I used to and I feel a lot happier knowing I don't have to worry about my phone. My family might start joining our meetings, and I might go on medication soon, too. I don't really want to go on medication, as I've never been on it before and I'm not too sure what the side effects are. But I'm willing to try anything to live a normal life. Overall, since I began seeing the new therapist I have felt much happier and more confident that I'm getting the right help to overcome my OCD.

Sophie was 17 when she wrote this essay. To read more of her story, see Part 1 on page 30.

I know one thing for sure: I haven't run across any person with OCD who hasn't been sensitive and caring, and it almost seems to be a curse because if we didn't care so much we wouldn't worry so much either. But there are a lot worse traits to have than sensitivity and caring, so embrace who you are while adopting coping methods for your symptoms of OCD.

Knowing my persistent thoughts were most likely considered obsessions, I started looking online every day, specifically searching for information about OCD. I related to so many of the more general symptoms and descriptions, but I wasn't sure I had the disorder. I would read a list of symptoms on one website and then compare that to another.

Getting to the bottom of my pain was *always* on my mind, even on Friday nights as my curling iron heated up. One night before I went out I found an article called "Thinking Bad Thoughts." I had finally found information that I *really* related to.

Although it was a few more weeks before I made an appointment with an OCD specialist, I felt empowered and more convinced than ever about what I needed to do next—reach out for help. I planned to find a psychiatrist or therapist, print out "Thinking Bad Thoughts," and hand it over with the hope that it might explain everything for me. But first I needed to find someone I could trust, and that would take some research.

CHAPTER 2

REACHING OUT

*"*When the disease is known
it is half cured.*"*

—Desiderius Erasmus

My obsessions had taken over my life. When I wasn't actively obsessing, I was thinking about why I was obsessing or how I could stop obsessing, and I constantly compared myself with others.

One night while Peter and I were visiting my friend Lauren in New York City—a vacation I had planned at a point when my obsessions weren't too intrusive—we went out to dinner with a group of her friends. I can't describe how badly I wanted to be "normal" and enjoy myself. Why was that so incredibly difficult? What had I done to warrant this torment? We were all adults out at a restaurant for adults, and I should have been able to take pleasure in their company. But just as I would slip into a carefree feeling, I would catch myself, almost as though I didn't deserve it. I would think, "I bet no one at this table has ever thought the things I've thought."

Seeing happy people made me feel less happy because it was in stark contrast to how I felt, and feeling unhappy reminded me of *why* I felt unhappy—because I had icky obsessions that stuck to my brain like chewed gum on the bottom of a rubber-soled shoe. No amount of scraping, coaxing, home remedies, or wishful thinking was going to get rid of the unwelcome guest.

One woman at the table was joyfully telling an animated story about her mother, her boyfriend nodding along in amused agreement, and despite my attempts at forgetting everything else around me and behaving and reacting like a "normal" person would, my thoughts devolved from your garden-variety (her mom must be so adorable!) to irrational and very OCD-ish (*she* isn't a mom and doesn't have little kids around, but she *has* a mom and even though she's an adult child to her parents now, she *was* a child, because all parents once had little kids in their care, and I bet *her* parents never thought the things I think or worried about hurting kids the way

I do). I glanced around the table, taking in the faces of my dinner companions: We were all children once. We all had parents who didn't hurt us. But was it because they never thought about it? Did they worry about it too but were able to move past the thoughts and not act on them?

How. Incredibly. Exhausting.

Before I left for that trip, it dawned on me that antidepressants might help me feel better. I didn't realize they could slow my obsessive thought track; I just reasoned that if I felt less depressed I might forget *why* I felt so terrible: the obsessions. Pretty roundabout, but I was willing to try. (I learned later that antidepressants *can* help with OCD—but only a doctor can tell you for sure if you need medication and what kind you need to treat your OCD.)

So one day at work, I tearfully emailed Mandi, one of my oldest friends, to ask her how I should go about getting a prescription. She was the best person I could talk to about the matter—not only is she a great listener and understanding friend, she's struggled with anxiety herself *and* works with mentally ill clients every day, advocating for their needs and making sure they're taking their medication.

Here's what I emailed Mandi. I was crying as I wrote it, but you probably wouldn't guess that from my casual tone. I added some observations from my point of view today in italics.

> I don't want you to worry about me too much, but I have a question. If I were to want an antidepressant would I need to see a psychiatrist or just a regular doctor? I've been really down [read: *I've been so depressed I never want to wake up because I'm afraid of what obsessions will plague me*] for over a month now and don't know what to do, and I'm confused [*true, I didn't know why I was having obsessions, but I knew exactly why I was depressed—because of the obsessions*] because I'm in love and am supposed to be happy. [*I felt enormously guilty that Peter was in love with me too and that I wasn't letting him into my whole world. But I knew (or thought) that if I told him the truth he would have no choice but to hate me and leave.*]
>
> Let me know what you think.
> Love,
> Ali

Even as I reached out for help I wasn't being honest about how badly I needed it. Take my advice, if you will: Don't put someone else's feelings above your needs, even if it means your parent* or friend or partner worries about you for a while. Be honest about what you're going through, at least to the point that whoever is in a position to help has a clear understanding of what you need and how much you need it.

Here is Mandi's reply:

Hi,

Some regular doctors will prescribe antidepressants but some will tell you that you have to go to a psychiatrist. I don't know what clinic you go to but there's probably a mental health clinic you can call. Unfortunately, it might take 1–3 months to get into a psychiatrist. If you find scheduling is way out you could call your regular doctor and see if she'll see you sooner based on that.

Anyway, you should talk to someone even though it's hard. It will likely help the situation and if not, what are you losing?

Feel free to call me tonight if you want to talk.

Love,
Mandi

P.S. I'm in love too and not supposed to be anxious!

Mandi's email was definitely encouraging, but I still felt unsure about making an appointment with a psychiatrist. Part of what scared me about asking for help was the possibility that nothing could help me. I couldn't bear the thought that medication or cognitive therapy (see page 59) might not make me feel better. I believed that if neither of those avenues worked, I would either be stuck with feeling depressed for the rest of my life (or what would feel like the rest of my life, no matter how long it may have actually lasted) or I would have to finally give in and kill myself.

With these fears clouding my judgment, I put off making an appointment and continued trudging through my life, waiting for the day I'd wake up magically cured. Instead I sank lower and lower

---

*You may live with one or two parents, or with a stepparent, foster parent, relative, guardian, or other adults. When I refer to your *parent* (or *parents*), I mean the family adult(s) who care for and about you at home.

into depression and moved from obsessing just about children to obsessing about family members.

Then one night I had what turned out to be a life-changing phone call with Mandi. I got up the nerve to tell her I had been obsessing about things, leaving out the more embarrassing details and describing instead how it felt to have the obsessions. I explained that if I didn't "finish" a thought it bothered me until I stopped everything and thought it all the way through. I couldn't stand it if a thought popped into my head and something interrupted it—I *had* to eliminate all distractions, sometimes by closing my eyes and

<u>Do You Have a Mandi in Your Life?</u> I feel particularly lucky to have had such a supportive person in my life, especially at such an incredibly difficult time.

You may not have someone *just* like Mandi, a mature friend who has knowledge of mental illness like she does, or someone you can trust with your deepest secrets, but you most likely have friends or family members who can be supportive.

Consider who you have confided in before and who has been a good listener. Think about how judgmental a person may be before you disclose everything about your symptoms or diagnosis. By no means do I think you need to hide anything about yourself or be ashamed of your disorder, but it's hard to divulge something personal to someone only to have that person make you feel worse about what you're going through. And since many OCD symptoms can seem pretty strange (which is probably why you haven't felt comfortable sharing them), not everyone will be able to understand.

While friends and family members may in fact be very compassionate, school counselors and social workers are *trained* to listen and keep information confidential. They'll give you a safe space to explain what's been going on in your life and can recommend what steps to take next—they likely have access to mental health resources that can take you even further than they can in your recovery process.

Go to page 45 for more on building a support network.

plugging my ears and letting myself think it through. I didn't tell her about the scary obsessions—those were an entirely different breed. Those I didn't want to think of for even a second or two, much less all the way through to "completion."

It didn't matter that I told Mandi bits and pieces. She heard enough and remembered enough to mention something critical in one of her emails: "Paxil is what people with obsessive-compulsive disorder go on," she said. "*Not* that you have OCD, but you just said you 'obsess' about things, so it could help."

(*Note:* Paxil is the brand name for paroxetine, which is actually one of several medications proven to work well for people with OCD. Read more about them in Chapter 4.)

It was the first time I had put two and two together. I had always considered myself an obsessive person, someone who dwelled on things, who couldn't let the tiniest things go. But I didn't realize that this could be categorized as an actual disorder. The idea made me optimistic; I was hoping I had a well-known mental illness because that meant I could be treated with medication and therapy. I found myself wanting to identify with symptoms of OCD.

I began researching OCD online. I found a great website for the International OCD Foundation, and it was there that I realized I could be helped. As I read the website I realized that I could be considered an obsessive-compulsive person, even without some of the compulsive behaviors. With my symptoms, I could be classified as a "pure obsessional." I don't wash my hands an excessive number of times; I don't have to count up to a certain number before I can leave my apartment; I don't drive around the block 10 times because I'm afraid I've run someone over and I need to make sure I didn't. I've learned that some things I've

International OCD Foundation
The International OCD Foundation (IOCDF) is a nonprofit organization founded by people with obsessive-compulsive disorder (OCD). The mission and goals of the IOCDF are to increase awareness of OCD, support research of the disorder, improve access to resources and treatment, and advocate for the OCD community.
www.OCfoundation.org
617-973-5801

done can be considered compulsions, like counting syllables on my feet, and even avoiding situations that could trigger obsessions, like a kid's birthday party—but I didn't know it then.

I was afraid that since I didn't have some of the more obvious compulsive behaviors such as repetitive hand-washing, I couldn't be diagnosed with the disorder. In fact, I thought I had something much worse that made me better suited for a life in prison or a candidate for sterilization, or that I had no identifiable illness at all and just had to live with myself as is—yikes. That felt scarier than running into an armed mugger in a dark alley.

But the only way I could find out what was really going on was to meet with a professional. First, though, Peter and I had that trip to New York to visit my friend Lauren.

ADVOCATING FOR YOURSELF

As the trip grew near, it became clear to me that I should stay home and call someone who could help me start feeling better. We had been planning that trip for months—Peter was especially excited because he had never been there before. But when the time finally came, I was so deep in my obsessive period that I knew I wasn't capable of letting go of any of my worries, large or small, and have fun. I wished I could be as happy as Peter was. I wished I could be excited about seeing my friend Lauren again. But I couldn't.

In retrospect, I should have cared less about the money we'd already spent, Peter's enthusiasm for the trip, and seeing Lauren. I should have advocated for myself. I should have told Peter that I was obsessing and that I needed to see a doctor. He would have understood.

Instead, we went. I pushed myself to be social, because I knew it would be unfair—and a total waste of the aforementioned money we'd already spent—to sit in the hotel room over the five days we were there. But I was miserable. By the end of our trip I was anxious, ready to get home and get help. Unfortunately, nothing went right on our trip back to Minneapolis. Bad weather in Chicago delayed our flight for two hours, so I had nothing to do but think about how badly I wanted to stop thinking.

Once we boarded, we were informed that our plane had a mechanical issue, so we sat for another 45 minutes. Peter and I held hands, and he gently rubbed my thumb with his own. I felt so unworthy of his love that I felt numb inside. I tried to distract myself by reading the in-flight magazine, but the brightly colored articles about exotic destinations only made me wish I could be carefree enough to take an interest in them. They reminded me of how unhappy I was because I couldn't find any joy in the prospect of travel or new cultures to explore. What was the point, really?

As much as I loved Peter and didn't want anything bad to happen to him, and as much as I knew my family would hurt if they lost me, and even though I knew I wasn't the only person on the plane, for a moment I thought that it wouldn't be so bad if we ended up crashing. It might have been the first time I had ever sat on a plane and didn't worry that something would go wrong. It would be so simple, really— I wouldn't have to take my own life and add that distressing element to my death; it would be done for me. Tragic, yes, but fairly cut and dried at the same time.*

Our flight arrived in Minneapolis safely, of course, but very late. There had been a large snowfall while we were gone. The cab dropped us off across the street from our apartment. We paid the driver, grabbed our heavy luggage, and trudged across the snowy street, where I hesitated.

"Where's your car?" I asked Peter.

He looked around and said, "I don't know." Then I noticed that my car was missing, too.

"Where's *my* car—did we get towed?" I asked.

Peter freaked out immediately. Our cars must have been in the way of the snowplow, so they both had been towed. I reassured him that everything would be all right as I unlocked the door to our apartment building, balancing my bag on my knee, trying not to drop it in the dirty snow on our front steps. I was upset, too; in fact, it was almost too much to take. But having our cars towed seemed like the least of my worries. I was too depressed to get worked up about the money and the inconvenience. I just wanted to lie down and sleep for days.

---

*OCD can lead to depression and thoughts of suicide. If you have such thoughts, please talk to a trusted adult right away or contact the National Suicide Prevention Lifeline (see page 13).

Getting Medicine and Other Help

Seeing a psychiatrist is the safest option, because psychiatrists have the special training to know what medicines to prescribe and what side effects to look for. Some people feel worse on medication—they might become angrier, sadder, or even have suicidal thoughts. If you are under 18, seeing a child or adolescent psychiatrist is recommended. If you can't get in to see someone soon enough, ask your general practitioner, family doctor, pediatrician, or other healthcare provider for recommendations. This person might be able to get you a faster appointment, prescribe medicine, and provide other types of support.

Once we found someone to bring us to the impound lot so we could release our vehicles to freedom, I called a psychiatric clinic to see if I could get in to see someone, as soon as possible. The trip and the disastrous homecoming had pushed me to get help, and I knew that at the very least I needed to be on medication. To my disappointment, the woman I reached not only said it would be months before I could get in, but she told me in an unkind tone of voice. I couldn't believe that I had waited so long and had been so picky about who to call only to be turned down, and somewhat rudely.

Since moving out of my parents' house I had seen dentists, eye doctors, dermatologists—but not a general practitioner. The only doctor I had regular appointments with was my gynecologist, so I mustered up enough courage to call her office to see if she could see me and prescribe me an antidepressant. She wasn't in, but a nurse was, and her response was the opposite of the intake person's I had just spoken to. This woman heard how shaky my voice was and how desperate I was coming across and said, "It sounds like you really need to see someone today."

She put me on hold for a bit while she made sure my gynecologist could see me later that day, and told me to hang in there. Her kindness and compassion made me even more emotional than I already was, but in a hopeful way. I knew someone cared, and that helped tremendously. Seeing my gynecologist for depression wasn't ideal, but I felt pretty desperate that day. Try not to wait so long to get help for yourself—that way you can get the best help sooner than later.

When I saw my gynecologist, I told her I'd been depressed and tended to obsess about things. I said I was hoping to go on Paxil because a friend of mine had told me about it and I thought it might help me. My doctor went through a depression checklist with me, and I answered yes to most of the questions (not to mention I was crying as we spoke). I didn't tell her I thought I might have OCD, and I couldn't summon the strength to tell her that my obsessions were about harming children—not when I was surrounded by pictures of babies she'd delivered hanging on her office walls. I figured she couldn't possibly understand.

(*Note:* Hindsight is 20/20. When I sought help I didn't know the right way to go about the process. Just because I did things a certain way doesn't mean I did them the right way. I am simply sharing my story, not step-by-step advice. See Getting Medicine and Other Help on page 42 for more information.)

She prescribed 10 milligrams a day, and I rushed to the pharmacy to pick it up. Since this was a new prescription for me, the pharmacist wanted to talk to me about it to make sure I understood how to take it and how it would work.

My eyes welled up with tears when she told me it could take six months until the medication made me feel normal again.

"Six months?" I said with despair—the poor woman was probably afraid of me. My balloon of hope lost a little air, but it hadn't popped. Later I swallowed my first pill with optimism. Spoiler alert: It didn't take six months until I felt better. Sure, it might have been that long before I felt a *lot* better, but I started noticing the changes pretty quickly. I felt calmer within a couple weeks, and I even embraced the side effects because I realized the medication was working. Go to page 76 to read more about how my medication worked for me and how I adjusted to it.

After all this time, I was finally on the road to feeling better. If I had advocated for myself sooner, I would have been further down that road.

FINDING A PSYCHIATRIST OR THERAPIST

Though I was feeling a little better, I still wondered if I had OCD. But I was still afraid to tell anyone about my bad thoughts, even my gynecologist. So even though I had reached out a bit and started on medication, I wasn't addressing the core of the problem. I kept visiting the International OCD Foundation website, doing more research, until eventually I found the "Thinking Bad Thoughts" article that clicked the light on for me. I was sure I had OCD, and I knew that I needed to see a psychiatrist or therapist.

I'll save you the agony of reading about the many ways I searched for someone who could help me—I had no idea what kind of professional was right for me. What if the person wasn't qualified? What if he was a kook? What if she had a policy of tough love, making me feel terrible?

Lucky for you, you don't have to replicate my several searches through the Yellow Pages or on Google. (Let's just say I wasted a lot of time, several weeks' worth, worrying that if I told anyone what I had been thinking they'd be obligated to turn me in to the authorities.) I found my psychiatrist on the International OCD Foundation website.

I live in a city, so there were several doctors listed in my area, and I chose mine because he was closest to my home. Yep, I picked the man who in many ways saved my life based on how many miles away his office was located from my front door.

Jon Grant, M.D. I wrote his name and phone number on a slip of paper, tucked it in my purse, and called from my office the next day.

I was surprised to hear Dr. Grant answer the phone himself. His voice was kind, professional, open. I nervously said, "Is this Dr. Grant?"

"Yes, it is," he said. "How can I help you?"

"I was wondering if I could make an appointment with you."

"Of course," he said. "I don't know when I have an opening in my schedule. If you feel comfortable, I can transfer you to the intake line."

There was something about his tone of voice that made me feel optimistic. So far, so good. He wasn't gruff or curt.

What If There Aren't Many OCD Professionals in Your Area? Until I
lived in Minneapolis, a fairly large city, I had no idea where to turn for
help. I feel for anyone who lives in a town or area that is a hundred
miles or more from an OCD psychiatrist, because it can make it very
difficult to get the right help.

It isn't hopeless, though. The first step you could take if you
don't know of any mental health professionals in your area,
particularly those familiar with OCD, is to use the care providers
database on the IOCDF website (**www.OCfoundation.org/
findproviders.aspx**). Enter the information requested to see if any
OCD specialists aren't too terribly far away.

Depending on whether you have a driver's license, your parents'
work schedule, and other factors such as finances and health
insurance, you may be able to work something out even if the only
OCD specialist is a few hours away. Maybe you will visit once a month
and fill in the gaps with phone calls. Some doctors in rural areas
travel to see patients who don't live near their practice (for example,
there is no dermatologist in the town I grew up in, so a dermatologist
from a bigger city practices out of the local clinic one day a week).

While it's usually best to meet with someone in person, don't
despair if that isn't an option. Some mental health professionals
conduct sessions over Skype, and researchers are evaluating a new
online treatment program called BT Steps. There's even an app called
Live OCD Free, created by an OCD therapist who engages her patients
in exposure and response prevention therapy (read more about
therapy in Chapter 3 on page 57).

If you can't find someone who specializes in OCD, look into
a psychologist, therapist, or mental health professional who
understands depression and anxiety on a more general level. You
might ask your regular doctor or school counselor if they know
anyone they can recommend. And if you can't find a therapist or
mental health professional you like or who seems to understand
what you are going through, look into online or local support groups
with others who have OCD. Try the IOCDF website, which links to

several groups, including teen groups, Christian groups, Jewish groups, queer groups, pure-O groups—and more.

You may find it helpful to join a group and talk about what you are going through, whether the members are your age or consist of all ages. Although at first you may think you only want to talk to other teenagers, you may actually benefit from a more multigenerational approach. Even though I'm only 34 (youngish compared to adults who are several decades older), I still offer a different perspective than another teen because I have been through many years of OCD troubles and am able to look back and see how far I've come, realizing that things *do* get better and nothing is completely hopeless. I may have bad days, but I know there will also be good days to come. Adults might offer advice or wisdom that comes from many years of experience.

If you don't find a support group, you can also try reading books that may help. I don't advise using a book or a support group as a replacement for professional help, but these avenues can certainly supplement your treatment (and could eventually serve as a substitute once you've met with someone to establish a diagnosis and a course of treatment) if your doctor doesn't specialize in OCD or is located too far away for regular appointments.

"Oh, okay," I said, still feeling a tiny bit desperate. "Do you happen to know how long your patients typically have to wait before getting in to see you?" I mentally crossed my fingers, hoping for good news.

"No, I'm afraid I don't," he said. "Call the intake line, and if it takes more than two weeks to get in, call me back."

Eek. More than two weeks? *More?* I didn't even want to wait one week. I felt desperate to get help. I didn't want things to get so bad that I wouldn't be able to get over it.

I called the intake line and was connected with a nurse who asked some questions I didn't feel totally comfortable answering at work, so I lowered my voice and spoke toward the wall, away from my door, as much as possible.

"I've been reading a lot about obsessive-compulsive disorder lately," I said. "And I think that . . . that might be me."

"Okay," she said. She seemed peppy. "I'll send along an OCD questionnaire for you to fill out, along with the usual paperwork."

Unfortunately, she told me I wasn't able to get in for another three weeks, but I didn't feel comfortable telling her I needed to get in sooner. Who was I, anyway? And I didn't want to call Dr. Grant back and be a nuisance.

I waited for another couple of days and then, after worrying that my condition might deteriorate beyond repair, decided it wouldn't hurt to call Dr. Grant personally again. I took my cell phone into the kitchen at work and shakily dialed his number. I was so delicate in those days, I would choke up and begin to cry at the slightest disappointment or kind word.

When Dr. Grant answered, I reminded him of our original phone call and said that I was hoping I could get in sooner than in three weeks.

"Tell me what's going on," Dr. Grant urged. I was trying to speak as quietly as possible in case any of my coworkers came into the kitchen and overheard me saying even one word, such as "obsessive."

"Well, I've been having some really bad obsessions the past couple of months," I said. "I think I might be obsessive-compulsive, and I just really need to talk to someone."

He was very apologetic when he told me that he only had office appointments on Mondays and Tuesdays, that he was very booked with appointments and just happened to be going to Boston to give a lecture the following week. I nodded as he spoke, scarcely aware that Dr. Grant couldn't see me over the phone line. I told him as confidently as possible that it was okay, that I understood he couldn't squeeze me in.

"I started on Paxil two weeks ago, and to be honest, I do feel a bit better already," I said as he apologized again.

"Oh, great," he said. "If you do start to feel like things are falling apart, please call me and I can try to help you over the phone."

As let down as I was that I couldn't get in to see him in person sooner, I knew I had made a good decision when I called Dr. Grant. He was already so understanding, so helpful. I still had a fear in the back of my mind that even he wouldn't be able to help me, that I'd have to relay my symptoms to doctor after doctor, until I felt completely drained and helpless. I reminded myself to keep hope.

It definitely helped that I hadn't even met my doctor yet and he was already more wonderful than I had hoped. Heck, I wasn't even his patient yet, and he was already willing to help me, even over the phone.

(Not all psychiatrists are like Dr. Grant, but that doesn't mean they don't care about your well-being. Go to page 45 to learn more about building a team of support.)

These good signs didn't exactly stop me from worrying about how the appointment would go. I still wondered if I had some *other* mental disorder. There was no way I was backing out now, however.

I was nervous for my appointment with the psychiatrist. I had waited weeks to make an appointment with somebody because I had actually thought that as I was telling the doctor about my obsessions, he would casually reach under the table and press a button

How Long Does It Take to Get in to See a Psychiatrist? The answer to that question can depend on many things, including where you live, what kind of insurance you have, and how old you are. You might call a clinic one day and be in to see someone the next week, or you may have to wait several months.

So what if you have to wait? What can you do in the meantime? One option is to see a general practitioner you can talk to about what you're going through. He or she may be able to offer some advice on how to cope with anxiety, recommend some reading materials, or prescribe medication. If you find a proper medication while you are waiting to see an OCD specialist, you may find a good measure of relief. You may even feel so much better by the time your appointment with the mental health professional finally rolls around that you'll find yourself reporting how great you feel and how bad your symptoms *used* to be.

Another option is to find a therapist or counselor first. Medicine usually works better when combined with counseling or therapy, and not everyone with OCD needs medicine to control it.

that would signal the police to come and arrest me, all the while nodding along knowingly.

When I received the OCD questionnaire in the mail, I was almost afraid to look at it. I read through all of the questions before I started marking anything down. I was surprised to find that although a lot of the questions didn't apply to me, especially things like hand-washing rituals, OCD symptoms were much broader than I had realized. I felt a huge sense of relief when I saw myself in some of the categories. I felt a twinge of hope that Dr. Grant could help me out, that he wouldn't judge me. I was glad that I would have words on paper that would precede my physical presence in his office; I didn't think I could bring myself to talk about my horrible obsessions, especially to a complete stranger.

After I finished answering the questions where the answers were as simple as circling numbers on a scale of 1 to 4, I struggled through the writing portion. I found that I could skip over a lot of the questions because the compulsive behaviors didn't apply to me. The night before my appointment I hesitated before I found the courage to write, "Being alone with children" as my worst fear, then sealed the envelope and hid it in a dresser drawer so Peter wouldn't see it.

MY FIRST VISIT WITH A PSYCHIATRIST

My appointment wasn't until four o'clock, so I had to go to work and sit in anticipation all day. I told a coworker that I had an appointment with a psychiatrist and how scared I was, and she told me she had seen one when her parents got divorced and that I wouldn't have to talk about anything I didn't want to.

"They're not going to judge you," she said. "Just think of all the horrible things they hear every day! You're normal." *Yeah*, I thought, *that's what you think*. I felt like I was pulling the wool over people's eyes and fooling them into perceiving me as a regular, everyday gal.

Dr. Grant's office was more like one of those you would find when you visit your general practitioner than the psychiatrist's office on TV and in movies. There was no leather fainting couch, no bookshelf-lined walls, no framed degrees hanging.

I sat in a small office-like chair as Dr. Grant thoughtfully paged through the questionnaire I had filled out. The silence was nerve-wracking—I watched him read through my answers, wondering when he'd recoil in disgust, but he never did. He only nodded now and then and scrawled notes on a pad. He assured me that the notes were for his personal use and that no one else would ever read them.

"All right," he said as he flipped through the last few pages. "Tell me why you're here."

I had been chewing gum on the way to the appointment because my mouth was dry, so I took a tissue out of the box on the desk beside me, wrapped my gum in it, and then clutched the bunched-up wad in my hand to absorb my nervous sweat.

"It's hard to talk about," I said, suddenly afraid I had waited all this time and wouldn't be able to tell my would-be savior what he needed to save me from. "I . . . I . . . let's just say the article I identified with was called 'Thinking Bad Thoughts.'"

"Okay, okay," he said, nodding along patiently. "There are three so-called taboo obsessions. They fall under the categories of religious, violent, and sexual obsessions. Would you say your obsessions fall into one of these categories?"

"Yes," I answered slowly. "Religious and sexual, but not violent. Maybe it's because I've always been so 'good' about sex. I wasn't going to have sex until I got married; I was always very into church."

I began to cry softly. Warm, salty tears were rolling down my cheeks and coming to a point on my chin, where they dripped off. I dabbed at them with my wadded-up, gum-filled tissue, then grabbed a clean one.

"I can't tell anyone because they'll stop loving me if they know." My throat tightened and another hot tear escaped my eye and began to roll down my cheek.

"I know it's easy for me to say, and I'm not telling you you have to tell anyone," Dr. Grant said, "but I am certain they would understand. They would still love you."

"Yeah, maybe my mom would," I choked out, feeling a bit more hopeful.

"You're not a bad person," he said in a convincing tone before he shrugged his shoulders and said, "Well, I don't know you. Maybe you are. Maybe you kick puppies or maybe you're a bad friend, but you're not a bad person because of this. What I've found about people with OCD is that they're some of the brightest people; they are very conscientious, so much so that they worry needlessly about things their morals would never allow them to do."

I had never thought of it that way. The reason my obsessions sent me into such a spiral of shame was that I *was* a good person, and I *did* have strong morals, I knew the difference between right and wrong, and I truly cared about doing the right thing. The people to worry about, Dr. Grant explained to me, are those who fantasize, rather than obsess, about violent behavior or taboo sexual acts like incest or molestation.

"It's almost as though whatever I think is the worst possible thing a person can be at that time of my life—that's what I believe myself to be." I struggled through my explanation, but Dr. Grant understood.

He nodded emphatically, sympathetically, as though he were saying, "Yes, yes, you're exactly right, this is what I've found in my research." I could tell I had hit on something that was common in OCD sufferers, which calmed me considerably.

After we chatted for a while longer, Dr. Grant made a teepee with his hands and said, "So what can I do for you? The answer, I think, is a lot."

I had never heard such sweet words. He could do *a lot* for me. A lot!

We talked about the therapy one of his colleagues uses. It sounded intense: one way to overcome a taboo obsession is to describe it in detail into a recorder, and then listen to it over and over again until it's no longer scary.

(See page 57 for more on therapy.)

As daunting as it sounded, I was willing to do the therapy if it would help me get better. He gave me the phone number of the therapist, but when I called the therapist a few days later, he said that while it was up to me whether I had therapy, the intensity of it could actually make me feel worse since I had already begun to improve on the medication I'd been taking for a few weeks already.

That was all I needed to hear. I did *not* want to get any worse, that was for sure. If I had started the therapy during the worst of my obsessive period, it would have had more benefit.

Based on my taboo obsessions, Dr. Grant recommended that I read *The Imp of the Mind* by Lee Baer, and we set up my next appointment. I left the session feeling a huge sense of relief. It may be one of the few times a person goes into a doctor appointment with symptoms and comes out of it happy to have a diagnosis!

You will likely need therapy or medicine, or a combination. Although I started with a doctor, many people start treatment by seeing a counselor or therapist first. Before scheduling, however, you (or your parents) should ask if the counselor works with patients with OCD. He or she can also help you with other problems you might have. If counseling alone is not helping, ask for a referral to a psychiatrist. And if you see a psychiatrist first, chances are he or she will refer you to a therapist to work on cognitive behavioral techniques and provide support. Your doctor or therapist will help you figure out what is most effective for you. The next two chapters discuss in detail the different kinds of therapy for OCD, how they work, and how they can help you.

SOMETIMES LABELS ARE A GOOD THING

Being diagnosed with OCD may feel like you've been stamped with a label, but you haven't. Your symptoms have a name, though, and in a way they've been bundled into a neat little package labeled obsessive-compulsive disorder.

It's not a label like a nametag that a person wears ("Hello, my name is Alison and I *am* OCD!") but more like a label on a file folder that contains lots of valuable information. When you need to organize your homework you probably keep each subject in a separate folder. That way you know what's in each folder and you know where to look when you need to access something. That's what being diagnosed with OCD is like—now you know what your symptoms mean and can use either "obsessive-compulsive disorder" or "OCD" as search terms to find helpful information on the Internet or in books. You can use the label to learn about treatment, read up on medication, and reach out to people who can help, either because they have OCD too or because they are professionals trained to help people like us.

Nicole's Story: Being Diagnosed Was a Relief

I always suspected that the way I thought and the actions I did were wrong or abnormal, but sometimes I thought to myself, "Maybe everyone does this, everyone thinks this." It wasn't until I was ending my freshman year in college that I knew for sure the way I functioned was not quite right. I was sitting in my Introduction to Psychology II class when we covered the subject of OCD. My professor started explaining symptoms and signs of OCD and I thought to myself, "Hmm, I really think that sounds like me, but I may just be being paranoid."

The professor asked the class if any of us knew anyone with OCD. I decided to take advantage of the opportunity, so I raised my hand and said that I knew a friend with OCD. I said, "She cannot wear certain colors of nail polish or things she considers 'new,' like if she recently bought the item. If she decided she wanted to wear her newly purchased nail polish, shirt, jeans, or anything else, she had a maximum of six hours. If she wore them longer than six hours, something bad could happen. She also told me that she has to blink every day 200 times in a row counting by fives, otherwise something bad might happen."

The professor said, "Oh, that is full-blown OCD."

I felt free. I felt like a weight was lifted off my shoulders because I was able to put a name and description to my obsessions and compulsions. I also felt horrible at the same time, thinking I was going to be stigmatized and ridiculed by family or friends if I were to tell them. I thought they might not believe me or might think I was crazy.

After that I tried to think about how far back I could trace my OCD. I traced it back as far as second grade, when I was afraid to change the clothes on my Barbie dolls because I believed something bad would happen if I did. I remembered after I watched *A Nightmare on Elm Street* the first time, I had to repeat to myself every day for several years "Not today, not tonight, not the next night" seven times while thinking of being safe so I wouldn't be murdered in my sleep. Luckily,

these symptoms have subsided over the years, but many
remain and many still arise.

After I realized what it was that I was experiencing, I
told my mom and she agreed to help me find a psychologist.
For three years now I have been seeing a psychologist and
receiving the help I need to reduce my OCD symptoms. I was
relieved when I went to my psychologist and she officially
diagnosed me. It was a relief to be diagnosed because I
realized I was not alone. With the help of medication and
my amazing psychologist and support system, my symptoms
subsided, especially those symptoms with new clothes and
"good" luck and "bad" luck.

I'm still getting better, and I still have some symptoms.
Whenever I cross a doorway I cannot think of a loved one,
with the fear that if I do, something bad will happen to that
person. For example, when I cross into my room I usually
think of an actor or actress so that my mind is not thinking
of my mom, dad, brother, boyfriend, or friends. If I were
to think of my mom and cross the doorway I would have
to step back out until I was able to clear my head, think of
an actor, and step through again. I'm always afraid that by
doing or changing something I might put the life of someone
I love in danger. This could mean switching to a new bottle
of shampoo, switching to a new ponytail, buying a new
bracelet, putting new jewelry on, getting new glasses, and
even simply wearing new eyeliner. Every day I struggle with
these obsessions of inanimate objects controlling my entire
world.

Some obsessions and compulsions are easy to hide, but
some really are not. It really bothers me when different foods
touch each other, so when it is dinnertime I usually have two
or three plates that have separate items of food on them. This
may seem trivial, but when you're at a family dinner and
are asking for two plates when one isn't even full yet, people
get puzzled. Whenever one of my parents leaves the house, I
have to keep saying "I love you" until the door closes behind
them and I am no longer able to say it with them hearing me.

I am afraid that when they leave home they may die and they won't know that I love them. Even if I just got into a huge fight with one of them, I will still say "I love you."

My most recently developed obsession and compulsion has to do with the bracelets I wear on my arms. I originally had one bracelet that I constantly wore, thinking it gave me "good" luck and protected me from bad things happening. Then one day I bought another and felt brave enough to put it on. Little did I know this would end up hurting me because now I am afraid to take it off. I then managed to somehow acquire five more along with the fear of taking them off. I have recently been able to successfully remove two without fear and am currently working on the others.

Without the love and support I get from the people around me, it would be very difficult to deal with my OCD. I have a wonderful mother who has helped me and supported me through this struggle and who has tried to understand the way I live my life. I have a wonderful brother who uses his sense of humor to ease my symptoms and make me realize how insignificant they really are. I have a wonderful boyfriend who challenges my OCD, making me face my fears whether I want to or not. Lastly, I have a wonderful psychologist who has been there with me since I was a teenager through difficult times. Without her guidance, support, knowledge, and connection I would still be drowning in my OCD. Luckily I am not, and with the right support and knowledge, OCD is a monster that can be beaten.

Nicole was 20 when she wrote this essay.

When you tell a therapist or counselor that you have OCD, this label helps this caring person as well. Professionals have many tools on hand, and when they know what they are working with they know what kits to put into action. A handyman wouldn't bring a toolkit of wrenches, hammers, nails, and the like if the job is to paint—he would bring paint, paintbrushes, drop cloths, and so on. Likewise, your ideal therapist won't show up for your session with tools meant for a different "project."

Labeling a folder doesn't make the contents go away, and so being diagnosed with OCD doesn't make the symptoms magically go away just because you know what you're dealing with, but now you know what to do with them. You can take action. I felt a lot better after being diagnosed, but I wasn't magically cured.

CHAPTER 3
HOW THERAPY CAN HELP

"What saves a man is to take a step.
Then another step."

—Antoine de Saint-Exupéry

According to the International OCD Foundation, it takes an average of 14 to 17 years from the time OCD begins for people to seek and get the right treatment. As sad as this fact is, it doesn't surprise me at all, because some symptoms of OCD are more obvious than others.

For example, if someone is so terrified of germs that he washes his hands over and over again, rubbing them raw, and spends an hour or more every day on bathing rituals, it will be clearer to his parents that something is wrong, and they will probably have an easier time learning that what's wrong is OCD.

In contrast, it took me so long to be diagnosed because it didn't occur to me that I had a treatable mental disorder. There's no "cure" for being gay. There was no pill to take to make me a better Christian. I couldn't check myself into treatment for being immoral. How was I supposed to know these were all symptoms of a treatable disorder?

Many of us, including myself, have obsessions that are "all in our heads"—not in the dismissive, you're-just-imagining-things way, but in the "pure obsessional" way. And those of us who have *any* type of OCD symptoms may feel ashamed of what we are going through and too embarrassed to tell anyone about it, even those who have the potential to help us the most. Believe me, I get it. Even when I learned what my symptoms meant, I still felt very hesitant to tell anyone about them. There was a fear in the back of my head that while I may have thought I had OCD, a doctor might think otherwise and the alternative diagnosis would be worse.

You might have felt the same way about your germ phobia, your checking rituals, or how you have to do everything an even number of times. Having any mental illness, not just OCD, is not like having a cold or the flu. The symptoms aren't always obvious, but by now, if you're reading this book, you probably have some inkling of what's going on and I hope you know where to turn for help, too.

The fact you're reading this book probably means you have either already been diagnosed or you have good reason to believe that you have OCD and are looking to this book for help and advice. Whether you have already seen a doctor or not, it can be enlightening to read up on different kinds of OCD treatment. It's good to keep in mind, though, that only a therapist or physician can diagnose OCD.

Therapy has been proven to help many people with OCD, and there are different kinds of therapy you can try. When you read the word "therapy," you might think of kicking back on a leather couch and talking about your childhood. But that is one specific type of therapy ("talk" therapy), and it's not as effective at treating OCD as cognitive behavioral therapy (CBT). CBT is the most common therapy for OCD, and there are some different types of CBT, but basically the idea is that the therapist helps you teach yourself to think a different way about things. *Thinking* differently helps you *feel* differently. The most effective type of CBT used for OCD is exposure and response prevention (see page 60). You'll read more about the types of therapy later in this chapter.

Your doctor should know what type of therapy will work best for your OCD symptoms, but if you need to try a few different avenues before you see improvement, don't feel too discouraged. It may seem like I'm simplifying matters, but it is *so* important to keep up hope. That doesn't mean you will never have moments of doubt (OCD is nicknamed the doubting disease, after all) or even moments of despair, but whenever you have the strength to do so, pull yourself up and remind yourself that there isn't just one way to feel better. Others have come before you and others will come after, and there are many people who have devoted their lives to helping people with OCD.

Only a licensed therapist can administer therapy. Your doctor or psychiatrist may recommend a therapist, but you are the one who needs to actually choose one. The International OCD Foundation recommends that when you are looking for a therapist, you ask the following questions:*

*Adapted from "How to Choose a Behavior Therapist" by Michael Jenike, M.D. Used with permission.

What techniques do you use to treat OCD? (Cognitive behavioral therapy or exposure and response prevention is a great answer.)

Do you use exposure and response prevention (ERP) to treat OCD? (This is the most effective type of therapy for treating OCD. You can read more about it on page 60.)

What is your training and background in treating OCD? (A CBT psychology graduate program, a postdoctoral fellowship in CBT, membership with the International OCD Foundation or the Association of Behavioral and Cognitive Therapists, or participation in specialized workshops or trainings are all good signs.)

How much of your practice currently involves anxiety disorders? (There's no magic percentage here, but the more experience they have, the better.)

Do you feel that you have been effective in your treatment of OCD? (Again, there is no right or wrong answer, but of course you want an effective therapist. Listen for a positive outlook and sound ideas.)

What is your attitude toward medicine in the treatment of OCD? (It's best to work with someone who's willing to prescribe medication or refer you to a psychiatrist, even if you ultimately do not take medication yourself.)

Are you willing to leave your office if needed to do behavior therapy? (An encouraging answer would be yes, since some of your obsessions or compulsions probably aren't contained to an office environment; for example, fear of public restrooms. However, since some therapists may be willing but unable to leave the office, don't entirely write off a therapist if the answer to this question is no.)

COGNITIVE BEHAVIORAL THERAPY (CBT)

"Security is mostly a superstition. It does not exist in nature. . . . Avoiding danger in the long run is no safer than outright exposure."

—Helen Keller

According to the International OCD Foundation, about 70 percent of people with OCD will see a 60 to 80 percent improvement in their symptoms after going through cognitive behavioral therapy. The most common type of CBT is exposure and response prevention therapy (ERP), but acceptance and commitment therapy (ACT) is a newer type of CBT that is gaining support.

Exposure and Response Prevention

The most effective type of cognitive behavioral therapy for OCD is exposure and response prevention (ERP). This therapy can be difficult to go through because you must face your obsessions head-on: you will be asked to confront the thoughts, images, objects, and situations that create anxiety (this is the exposure part of the equation) and then decide *not* to perform the compulsion you normally use as a coping method (response prevention). You will repeat this until you don't feel as anxious about not doing it. You will eventually see that, for example, reciting the same prayer exactly 10 times has no bearing on the well-being of your loved ones—because when you don't do it, they are all still alive and well.

In ERP you may be asked to do any of the following assignments, depending on your obsessions or compulsions and what makes the most sense for you: writing, reading, looking things up on the Internet, listening to recordings that you or the therapist make up, going to places or being around people that make you nervous, touching things you usually avoid, breaking rules you made up for yourself, making up signs that contradict your obsessive beliefs to hang in your room, agreeing with uncomfortable thoughts, saying or writing names, words, or numbers that make you anxious, or throwing away things that you have been hoarding. Basically, ERP is a way of convincing your brain that nothing bad will happen if you stop paying attention to obsessive thoughts and engaging in compulsive behavior.

You can see why this type of therapy can be so hard: You are being asked to confront fears that you have spent weeks, months, or even years building up in your mind so that they have become very powerful to you. But as with many things in life, what's best for us isn't always easy. That goes for exercise, eating well, ending an unhealthy relationship with a person we love, studying, and making ethical decisions. If you are engaging in ERP and find it difficult, imagine the alternative—continuing to live in fear and being held back by your obsessions and compulsions. Try your best to look toward the light at the end of the tunnel. You might want to compare it to exercise: If you're sweating and your muscles are burning, it would feel pretty good to stop the workout. But it feels great to see the result of the exercise, whether that is better endurance for fun activities, a flatter stomach, or bigger muscles.

You might be thinking, "But, Alison, you didn't go through ERP. Who are you to talk?" You're right. I didn't, because the therapist I spoke with said that since medication had already made me feel better ERP might actually make me regress instead of improve. And trust me, I didn't want *that* to happen. I'll be honest, I can't even imagine uttering my worst fears into a tape recorder, or even detailing them to one other person, and having to listen to them over and over again until they are more boring than scary. I understand how hard it would be. If you go through ERP, no matter how intensive it is or how long it lasts, you have my respect.

Although I didn't go through ERP, I would have done it in a heartbeat if my doctor had strongly recommended ERP for me. That's because I know it works. Decades of research have shown this to be true, and have shown the pain of OCD to be worse—and to last longer—than the pain of ERP.

And the truth is, even though I didn't go through formal ERP, I wouldn't be better now if I hadn't in fact faced my fears in much the same way people do in ERP. I worked hard to retrain my brain using a combination of recommended techniques—basically an informal version of ERP. You can read about that on page 65.

Robert's Story: Exposure and Response Prevention Therapy Helped Me

I was first diagnosed with OCD when I was in third grade. At that time, I had a bunch of weird symptoms. They popped up at school, but never at home, so my parents didn't know about them. My mom recognized my OCD as such when our family was on vacation—my leg brushed up against hers, and I felt the need to repeat it with the other leg. I almost tripped her when I tried. It was kind of hard explaining it to her, but fortunately, she had heard about the disorder on the radio and suspected I had OCD.

My mom started taking me to cognitive behavioral therapy. I've been told it was very hard to find a good therapist, but we eventually did. I think it was an organization called OCD Chicago that finally helped us.

We did exposure and response prevention—gradually exposing me to the things that triggered the obsessions, with me then fighting the urge to perform the compulsions. We started off slow, tackling the easy ones first.

My therapist and I did bizarre things, but they were quite effective. When I had a compulsion to turn multi-toggle light switches on and off simultaneously, we attached a set of light switches to a block of wood and my therapist had me turn them on and off one at a time. I also had an obsession with raw wood—I was afraid I'd get splinters—so another exercise was rubbing my hand over raw wood.

The hardest compulsion I had to overcome was backward talking. When I said or heard something, I almost always felt the urge to repeat it backward, either under my breath or mentally.

This was a difficult compulsion to overcome. Not only was it particularly strong, but if I repeated something in my head, there was no way for my parents or therapist to hear it. I had to report my urges and their intensity on the honor system. Despite the importance this compulsion played in my life, I can hardly remember the therapy I performed for it. I believe it may have involved repeating things forward instead of backward, or it may have simply involved stopping myself from repeating anything at all. Either way, it was eventually bested like the others, and it was a big load off my shoulders.

It wasn't easy to overcome my obsessions, but in time, I became very adept at doing so. Today, my compulsions hardly ever get in the way of my day-to-day life. I still have a therapist, and we meet from time to time.

> The best advice I could give to someone with this disorder is to stick with the treatment. Do the exercises your therapist assigns, and you will see changes. Therapy is far from easy. Often, the urge to perform a compulsion can be nearly over-powering. With time, however, you will start to see changes, to the point that you simply recognize the compulsion and resist it as a matter of course. Therapy does work.

Robert was 21 years old when he wrote this essay.

Acceptance and Commitment Therapy

Since acceptance and commitment therapy (ACT) is such a new form of therapy for OCD, not as much research has been conducted and it's not yet known exactly how effective it is. If your doctor recommends ACT for you, it may be after you've already made progress with ERP, and you might even engage in ERP and ACT at the same time.

ACT is all about accepting that we all think "bad" thoughts now and then. Part of being human is feeling a wide range of emotions and coming across many different ideas and experiences, and they're not all positive. It's important to accept that you don't have control over the thoughts that enter your mind—you can only control how you respond to those thoughts. (For more information on OCD and ACT, go to www.ocfoundation.org/EO_what_is_act.aspx.)

I didn't know it at the time, but one very helpful coping technique I used after my diagnosis was similar to ACT. When an obsessive thought popped into my head, I immediately responded with "It's just a thought. It doesn't mean anything. Everyone thinks thoughts like that, but they don't freak out about it." It was a great reminder that I wasn't a bad person and the only difference between me and someone without OCD is that I let my oddball what-if thoughts take over. This sort of self-therapy, in this case a technique I read about in a book by Edna Foa and Reid Wilson called *Stop Obsessing! How to Overcome Your Obsessions and Compulsions*, was one of a few I engaged in to get better.

How Long Do I Continue with Therapy? You might go through some period of therapy during which you will learn techniques for coping with your anxiety. If you undergo exposure response prevention therapy you will be exposed to your fears until they aren't scary any more, or at least to a point where you can take over on your own time.

Is that the end of it? It all depends on what kind of problems you have, how helpful you find therapy to be, and how your family is handling the costs. It's a decision you, your therapist, and your parents can make together. If you are doing well, there may be basic financial reasons to stop or cut back on the therapy. On the other hand, if the cost of therapy is workable for your family, you may *want* to continue meeting with a therapist to talk through everyday issues as well as anything OCD-related you're going through. Even after I felt tons better and was pretty darn capable of coping with my OCD symptoms when they happened to pop up now and then, I still found it helpful to see my psychiatrist once in a while.

Touching base with someone who grounds you can be beneficial, and there is certainly nothing wrong with continuing therapy. And, of course, if you have relapses over time you can get professional help again, this time knowing what to expect. As with medication, you should continue with the regimen that works for you. The road to fewer symptoms and a life that is less weighed down by OCD might be long and slow, and that is okay! Really, truly. There are so many experiences and goals in life that take hard work to achieve, and the journey can be rocky and pleasant at different junctures. And there is nothing you have to do—this is your life, and you should do whatever works for you and makes you your personal best.

FACING YOUR FEARS ON YOUR OWN

"Do the thing you fear and the death of fear is certain."

—Ralph Waldo Emerson

Sometimes you don't choose therapy—therapy is forced upon you. I don't exactly mean that an authority figure will drag you kicking and screaming to see a psychiatrist (although you may not want to go, and your parents might require you to anyway). I mean that sometimes you are forced into facing the very fears you have been working so hard to avoid, and that's what therapy for OCD is really all about: facing fears.

That's what happened to me. I did not do formal ERP therapy, but life conspired to force me to face my fears.

I had gotten to the point that I was absolutely terrified of being alone with children, which wasn't too hard from a practical perspective because I didn't have kids, most of my friends didn't have kids, I wasn't a teacher or nanny, and I didn't have any nieces or nephews. I just had to struggle through the times, few and far between, when I did have to be around kids. Even when I was feeling much, much better and had been on medication for about a year and a half, I still didn't like the idea of being around kids. I just kept hoping and praying my married brother Brent would keep putting off having kids of his own, hoping he was like me in that he enjoyed being somewhat free and independent, but I knew his wife was looking forward to getting pregnant and it was only a matter of time.

That didn't make me feel any less shocked when my brother came over one night and told me the news: They were expecting a baby. I feigned excitement and congratulated him. As my husband, my brother, and I stood in our kitchen, talking about the big announcement, my brother said, "It's kind of scary." My husband dismissed this with a hearty, "Nah, people do it all the time!" while I stood there thinking, "Yuh-uh, it's scary!"

I congratulated Brent again, but once he was gone, Peter and I sat on the couch and I cried. The words I said out loud were, "I'm afraid I'll fall in love with the baby and then want a baby, but I don't want a baby," which was partly true. But my bigger fear, of course, was that this meant I would *have* to be around a baby now, this would be my niece or nephew, and how could I explain that I wouldn't help out? The clock was ticking; Brent and Kim had waited several months to tell anyone about the pregnancy, and the baby was due in just a few more months.

The day my darling nephew Eli was born, I did feel afraid. But I also couldn't wait to meet the little guy—and that anticipation won out. I was the first person at the hospital. I held my nephew, unfolded his blanket to get a better look at him, removed his cap to see his shock of dark hair, and changed his tiny little diaper.

I was in love, and all of this contact in the presence of his parents helped, but I was definitely still worried. Eventually they would ask me to babysit him, alone. I visited as much as possible to just hold him and rock him, and soon the time came—they asked me to watch him for three whole hours.

I was worried enough that I invited a coworker over to see Eli, and that really helped me. Somehow I got through the three hours and was able to get him to sleep, all without harming a hair on his precious head.

Eli is now five years old. We have been extremely close since he was a baby, and we love each other to pieces, and I've been blessed with another nephew, Asher, who's now three years old. Over the years I have changed countless diapers, wiped their snotty noses, driven three hours with just the two of them in the car with me—an especially difficult task, as I couldn't stop picturing an accident on the freeway—rocked them to sleep, lay down with Eli in his bed (and once with Asher in his crib), and just about everything in between.

Spending so much alone time with my nephews as their number one go-to babysitter meant facing my fear of being alone with children, over and over and over again. It certainly wasn't easy, but I pushed through my doubts, tackling them one at a time—kind of like a ninja surrounded by enemies, come to think of it. I feel proud to say my nephews are in good hands when I am in charge of their well-being, and I haven't had intense fears about harm coming to them, at least not at my own hands, for years. This doesn't mean those thoughts never creep in—but it does mean I am able to brush the thoughts off and remind myself I am their loving aunt who would protect them at any cost.

About a year ago I was helping Eli into his pajamas after a bubble bath, and as I buttoned his top he said, "I can take care of people."

Surprised and charmed by this out-of-the-blue statement, I said, "Yes, you can take care of people. Can I take care of people, too?"

His response still makes me smile: "You *do* take care of people."

He was right. I do take care of people. Quite the opposite of what I had for so long worried myself capable of, that I could actually bring harm to people. Somehow I've always known this about myself, that I am a caring, nurturing person—and the fact that I am is a big factor in my OCD—but until I faced my fears head-on I couldn't know for sure. That's why cognitive behavioral therapy is so important and helpful in the treatment of OCD. Until a person who's afraid of the dark gets through a scary night and comes out unscathed, he might always be afraid of the dark. Until a person who's afraid of spiders lets one crawl across her hand without it biting her and causing her harm, she might always be afraid of spiders. And if I had never become an aunt, I might still believe that children should steer clear of me.

I was basically engaging in "therapy" just by living my life in a way that often felt very uncomfortable. Although this worked for me, I had already been on medication and seeing my psychiatrist in short talk sessions for several months before my oldest nephew was born. While your ultimate goal is to engage in a regular routine in which you might come across the very situations you fear the most, you may need to work toward that goal under the watchful guidance of a therapist.

My psychiatrist likened a therapist to a personal trainer at the gym—while you might have the drive to exercise on your own, a personal trainer can push you beyond your limits, tailor your regimen to your unique needs, and hold you accountable. A therapist will encourage you to try things you don't think you're capable of, and will be there supervising so you feel safer.

Here's a suggestion for doing some self-therapy in order to face your fears—maybe after you've met with a psychiatrist or therapist or started a medication. Once you're feeling a little better, try to place yourself into a situation you would normally avoid. For me it was babysitting my nephews; for you it might be using a public restroom, leaving a room without turning the light on and off several times, or doing a homework assignment just once without going over it with a fine-tooth comb.

"I DON'T WANT TO GO TO THERAPY"

I was visiting my parents one weekend and my mom and I went on a walk through our neighborhood, something we have always enjoyed doing together, even in the dead of winter.

As we were walking along a dark, rural road, a car approached us from behind. We moved out of the way a bit, and then my mom unexpectedly pushed me into the ditch as the car passed by! I was understandably shocked and a little annoyed. Who does that? Apparently my mom, that's who.

"I'm sorry!" she said. "I just panicked."

My mom had pushed me into the ditch to keep me out of harm's way—her maternal instinct had kicked in.

So what does this have to do with treatment for OCD? As much as you want to get better, you might not want to go to treatment. Or maybe you're willing to see a therapist once or twice but you're appalled at a doctor's or parent's suggestion that you start a long-term program or even check into a residential program. The adults in your life might be trying—metaphorically, of course—to push you into a ditch to make sure you aren't hit by a car.

If your parent or another adult in your life is urging you to do something you're not comfortable with, ask yourself why. Most likely it's because that person has your best interest at heart. Your parent—or counselor, sibling, or other family member—is pushing you to challenge yourself so you can get better. If you're not sure, ask another adult you trust for a second opinion. Most important of all, look inside yourself. Are you avoiding therapy because it's scary, or because you really don't think it will help? Is your parent pushing you because she or he wants to see you improve?

Even if you end up hating the therapy you undergo or it isn't as effective as hoped, don't give up on treatment. It isn't one-size-fits-all. Everyone is different. Try to keep an open mind when you meet with your therapist. Don't be afraid to ask questions, or to be honest about how you feel about the suggestions the therapist gives you. Also, for therapy to work, you have to feel comfortable with your counselor. It's okay to ask if you can see a different therapist, but think about your reasons for doing so.

If you are worried about your first appointment or two, by all means, have a loved one join you. Peter went to an appointment with me to better understand what I was going through—you could have a parent or another relative join you. Not all parents will understand, but you need to get help and should seek it out where you can. There may come a time in intensive treatment when you have to go it alone (with the therapist, of course), but having this support in the beginning can build a solid foundation for success.

CHAPTER 4
HOW MEDICINE CAN HELP

"I have made peace with medication, coming to understand how it helps me function, and thereby helps me serve my greater good."

> —Jeff Bell, in his book *Rewind, Replay, Repeat: A Memoir of Obsessive-Compulsive Disorder*

My life is pretty great now, and I owe much of that to taking an antidepressant. It eased my anxiety and boosted my mood enough that I felt more confident to take on my obsessions. The medication calmed my brain's constant hiccup-like activity so eventually I was able to calmly and rationally address each thought. I've been taking medication for eight years now, and it's as much a part of my daily routine as brushing my teeth—but even easier. I went from distressing all the time, even while lying on the couch in front of the TV, to enjoying life again.

Will medication help you, too? It's very likely. Medication has been shown to benefit about 70 percent of people with OCD, and those people will see a 40 to 60 percent reduction in their OCD symptoms.

Medication can play a big role in reducing OCD-related anxiety and lifting a person out of depression, but antidepressants (which are commonly used with OCD) aren't for everyone, especially teenagers. If medication is recommended, don't hesitate to ask questions about what the medication is, how long it takes to work, what risks are associated with it, and if there are other ways of treating OCD. Some teens may want to try therapy first, while others' symptoms are so severe they may want to try medicine first.

If you are prescribed an antidepressant as a teenager, you will see a "black box warning" issued by the FDA. Antidepressants may sometimes increase suicidal thoughts and urges in teenagers—pretty much the opposite of what they're supposed to do—and it is particularly risky when you first start taking them. While very serious, these side effects rarely happen, so take your medication in good faith and with optimism, armed with the very important knowledge that you should *immediately* tell someone, especially an adult you live with (like a parent) and your doctor if you do begin to feel suicidal.* That way you can get help and switch medications if needed.

FINDING THE RIGHT MEDICATION

Although you may not be depressed, if your doctor prescribes medication it will almost certainly be an antidepressant. Studies have shown seven antidepressants to be effective for treating OCD in teens (brand names are in parentheses):

- fluvoxamine (Luvox)
- sertraline (Zoloft)
- citalopram (Celexa)
- escitalopram (Lexapro)
- fluoxetine (Prozac)
- paroxetine (Paxil)
- clomipramine (Anafranil)

Now, that doesn't mean you could take any one of these medications and it would be effective for *you.* All you need is one, but it may take some trial and error, and your doctor may combine an antidepressant with another medication, such as an antipsychotic medication. (Don't let the name scare you! It's not just prescribed to people who are psychotic; it also helps with the obsessive thinking associated with OCD.)

Most antidepressants work by targeting neurotransmitters, especially serotonin, norepinephrine, and dopamine, each in a different way. When these neurotransmitters are balanced, your brain cells are better able to send and receive the chemical messages that can

---

*If you can't find the immediate help you need, call the National Suicide Prevention Lifeline (1-800-273-8255) or go to their website for a live chat (suicidepreventionlifeline.org).

boost your mood and prevent that broken record of thoughts OCD causes. Medications that work by blocking the reabsorption of serotonin to help balance it are called selective serotonin reuptake inhibitors (SSRI). Anafranil, the most thoroughly researched medication for OCD, is the only medication listed previously that is *not* an SSRI.

In recent years, researchers have found some evidence that it might be helpful to target another chemical, glutamate. Studies have shown that abnormal levels of this chemical may contribute to OCD. Stay tuned for new drugs on the market; if you don't find the relief you need with currently used antidepressants, you may benefit from the newest cutting-edge medication.

You should always take your doctor's advice, but it's a good idea to do some research on meds before your doctor writes a prescription. Your path to wellness should be a collaborative effort—and involving yourself in the decision-making process may help you stick with your treatment plan.

Kiersten's Story: It Took Time to Find the Right Medicine for Me

At the end of my junior year in high school, I fell into a deep state of depression, agitation, and self-loathing. During those months I had two emotional breakdowns, and my mother decided I ought to see a psychiatrist and start taking some medication to alleviate my constant symptoms.

After seeing the psychiatrist and telling him my symptoms, we learned that I had OCD. I was prescribed medicine and took my first dose the next day in the morning. I knew exactly when the medication "kicked in," because I suddenly felt very strange in class and my eyelids began to flutter. This really scared me, and that made it worse, so part of the reaction may have been psychosomatic. I automatically began to assume I would have to go to the hospital, not really knowing that it takes time for the body to get used to these types of medications. When this happened, I was playing in the school orchestra. I had to stop what I was doing and go see the teacher, who also noticed that my pupils were dilated and bloodshot. For the rest of the day, I felt jittery and high.

I experienced a lot of twitching and cold, tingling sensations on various parts of my body.

That night, I couldn't sleep, and the day afterwards, I didn't go to school because I could hardly stand up straight, I was weak, my head felt heavy, and I had chills. For the rest of the week, I began to feel better but still did not feel quite right. My anxiety had increased and constantly felt like I had an internal chill. I would also have bouts of hard shaking.

After all of this, my psychiatrist gave me a new medication to take. But I refused to try it. In fact, the reaction I had with the first medication scared me so much that I was afraid to take *any* sort of medicine—even over-the-counter meds I had been taking my whole life. I feared that if I took *any* type of anxiety medication it would make me crazy or kill me. I did a large amount of research on the Internet about the new medicine he had suggested; researching was one of my many compulsions. I continued to worsen. I developed many strange anxiety symptoms, such as depersonalization, and seemed to develop bizarre new obsessions almost every week. At last, later that winter, I had reached rock bottom. I knew that I had to stop telling myself that my disorder would go away and do something to make it better.

In the middle of March, my psychiatrist chose a new medication for me, and told me I had to take it if I wanted to start feeling any better. Though it took a few days for my body to get used to the medication, it was overall very gentle and I did not experience any of the adverse effects I had when I took the first medication he'd prescribed. Within a week, my life was already much better. I remember I was at work one day and suddenly realized that I had not been dwelling on all of my obsessions as I used to all of the time. I could think much more rationally and no longer had any of my old anxiety symptoms.

Not only has it greatly diminished my anxiety and OCD, but it has also caused me to gain a great deal of weight. I have been underweight my whole life. Ever since I was nine years old, I fluctuated between 75 and 80 pounds. This was not because of an eating disorder but possibly because of a hyperactive metabolism or thyroid. A few months after starting to take my new medicine, I had already gained 10 pounds, which I was very happy about.

Now, a year later, I am proud to say I weigh over 100 pounds and still feel exponentially better than I did before I started taking medication. The only complaint I have is that I experience a lot of drowsiness, particularly in the middle of the day or in the early evening and often have to take a nap. Sometimes this messes up my sleeping schedule and interferes with doing schoolwork. Taking this risk and trying the medication was a big leap of faith for me, but I did it, and it is one of the best decisions I have ever made in my life.

Kiersten was 17 years old when she wrote this essay.

Medication can turn lives around and is often the first step toward battling OCD. For some people it's the best solution to their problems. Untreated OCD can make even regular routines feel overwhelming, and the antidepressants known to work on OCD symptoms help you obsess less, giving you more confidence to talk about your symptoms or start cognitive behavioral therapy. It may not be the last step you take in treating your OCD, but it can build a solid foundation for success.

I often visit an OCD support page on Facebook, where people with OCD ask questions and share advice. One day someone asked what meds are best for OCD. Someone answered with specific drug names and another said "None." It was his opinion that since he doesn't take medication, no one else needs to either, and that only therapy works for OCD. I'm no expert, but I didn't feel right about leaving that response unanswered. It can be dangerous to listen to just one person's opinions because that person could be uninformed, biased, or unstable. So I just noted that everyone is different and told the person who had posted the question that she would need to see a medical professional to figure it out. Medicine is not right for everyone, but it is for many, and that shouldn't be denied.

SIDE EFFECTS

While taking medication ultimately had wonderful positive effects for me—I'm not depressed, I hardly ever obsess, and I no longer have anxiety stomachaches—I experienced somewhat unpleasant side effects for the first few weeks.

My psychiatrist might disagree with me, but I think I experienced a placebo effect when I started taking my medication. Looking forward to fewer obsessions and allowing myself to hand some control over to a medication relieved some of my anxiety. Not all of my energy was going toward stopping the obsessions anymore. Some of it was going toward thoughts of a better life, and I didn't feel such a heavy weight on my shoulders. The medication would take some of the pressure off and start working, even if bit by bit, pill by pill, to reconfigure my brain. Just knowing that helped a lot.

Almost right away I had a dry mouth and felt thirsty no matter how much water I drank, and I tried to increase my flow of saliva by chewing gum and sucking on sour candy. I felt tics in my brain, like little electrical shocks, and I yawned a lot, often jerking involuntarily as I worked through the yawns.

One funny (but sometimes frustrating) side effect has been the onslaught of anxiety dreams I have nearly every night. It's almost as though my medication and brain retraining helps me get through each day without anxiety holding me back, but it needs to come out somehow.

The most frustrating side effect in the beginning was fatigue. I felt extremely exhausted for the first several days that I was taking paroxetine. I could have fallen asleep sitting up if I hadn't fought hard not to do so, and at night my body felt tired enough to sleep heavily, but my brain was going a mile a minute—not with obsessions, but with those little tics—and just when I would start to doze off in a comfortable position, my legs or arms or feet or hands would jerk out of place. I could *not* fall asleep and stay asleep in the same position even though I desperately wanted and needed the rest.

I also gained weight. I should say a few things about this side effect. If you gain weight, don't be hard on yourself about it. It happens. Not all antidepressants that help OCD symptoms cause weight gain, but paroxetine has been shown to. After I put on the pounds, I went on message boards and was horrified to see how many people posted about gaining weight. But Dr. Grant told me that although it is shown to *cause weight gain,* it is *not* shown to *prevent weight loss.*

As a woman who had always been pretty effortlessly thin, the weight gain was hard for me. It was only about 10 pounds at first, but it bothered me. I *needed* to know that my medication wouldn't keep me from losing weight, so I went on a rather strict diet and—believe it or not—got sort of obsessive about it all. I meticulously counted my calories and even broke into tears one night when Peter added an ingredient to our dinner that wasn't listed in the recipe. I did lose weight, but I had been so strict with myself that as soon as I started to let up a bit I started to gain it back.

Paroxetine reportedly makes people who take it crave carbs. I'm not sure if that was true for me or not, but I can tell you for sure that before I went on the drug I had near-constant anxiety-related stomachaches. I hardly ate anything, ever. No wonder I had been thin! I never knew that other people didn't get cramping pains in their gut every time they ate lunch or breakfast, or before a meeting or first date, or before work or school every morning. What a wonderful little side effect! Now I could eat whatever I wanted, and I did—which is probably the real reason I gained weight. I hadn't eaten with such abandon since I was a little kid, and even then my tummy was too small to really enjoy it. For years I had thought I was lactose-intolerant, but it turns out that dairy on top of my already queasy stomach was just too much. Even vegetables and fruits used to make my stomach churn. Now I felt fine after eating most anything, and it made other aspects of my life more enjoyable—dinners out with friends, picnics, parties, dates, movies at the theater, road trips—all that good stuff.

If you gain weight after starting your medication and it really bothers you, you can talk to your doctor about switching meds. My psychiatrist didn't want to switch mine, and I was okay with that. Ultimately, maintaining a healthy weight requires eating as well as you can most of the time, eating less-healthful foods in moderation, and exercising—this is true no matter the reason for your weight gain, unless you have a more serious health issue that needs to be addressed. Again, if you have tried everything and the scale won't budge (and neither will your pants zipper), talk to your doctor. I decided that although I didn't like the extra fat I was carrying around my waistline, it was a minor inconvenience compared to being depressed and obsessive. Overall I was happier, and I wouldn't sacrifice that for being 10 or 20 pounds thinner.

Some people lose weight on antidepressants, too, but only one of the medications listed on page 72 notes weight loss as a side effect: fluoxetine (Prozac). If you are already slim, losing weight could make you underweight. If this happens, talk to your doctor about how to gain weight with *healthy* habits, not with processed, high-fat foods and sugary drinks.

I've found that the best way to deal with side effects, especially the ones that seem to be directly targeting the brain, is to view them as little hurdles to overcome on your way to recovery. Many side effects, such as nausea, drowsiness, fatigue, and blurred vision, last only a few weeks. If you've started medication, it may not have fully kicked in yet, and you're probably still having obsessions and performing rituals, but *something* is going on in that complex brain of yours, and that ain't all bad.

WORRISOME SIDE EFFECTS

Having said that, there are some side effects of antidepressants that aren't okay and mean your medication isn't working properly. If you experience any of these, tell someone immediately, preferably a parent or another trusted adult *and* your doctor. If you never thought of suicide before but now you are thinking it seems like a valid option, or your thoughts of suicide have increased and are more persistent, it may be a side effect of your antidepressant. Either way, if you are considering suicide at all, tell someone *right away*. If it is due to your medication, your doctor can help you get off that medication and start something new, and if it isn't, it's still really important for you to talk to someone and work through these feelings.*

Sometimes people are afraid to ask for help because they might be checked into a hospital or psychiatric clinic. It's possible this will happen if you tell your doctor about your suicidal thoughts, but it's really important for your safety and health that you not let that deter

*See the note on page 13 for more information.

you. If you do need longer-term help, you will be in professional hands. And just think—it will take some of the burden off of you. You will be better able to rest and let your medication or therapy work for you. Every step you take carries you toward recovery.

PAYING FOR MEDICATION

There are many factors involved when it comes to the cost of medication—although I've taken the same medication at the same dose for several years now, the cost of it has gone up. Some of the reasons are more obvious than others: the brand-name version will generally be more expensive than the generic equivalent (unless your insurance for some reason favors the brand and you get it for less), but there are other factors that might be less obvious.

For example, depending on where you get your prescription filled, the pills might only come in certain doses. Your prescription might be for 30 milligrams, but your pharmacy may not provide 30-milligram pills and you will have to take three 10-milligram pills or one and a half 20s. However, another variable for cost is that some pharmacies offer an incentive for filling three months' worth of your prescription at once, or for having your pills delivered to your door.

You might not think much about it right now if you are covered by your family's insurance plan; you can talk to your parents about their coverage and what works best for them and you.

Someday, if not already, you will be on your own and in charge of your own medication (and everything else in life), and you may run into some roadblocks. If you have problems with insurance coverage or medication costs, continue to communicate openly with your doctor to see what can be done, and ask about the free samples drug companies deliver to clinics. In my early 20s I had a doctor who loaded me up with samples every time I left her office. I didn't have to pay for that prescription for months. Pharmacists can be very sympathetic and helpful as well, so don't hesitate to make them aware of your situation and get their advice.

Another option is to contact the manufacturer of your medication, because they often have programs to help patients who can't afford to buy it. (Have you ever noticed that little message at the end of some prescription drug commercials? "If you can't afford your medication, Pharmaceutical Company Inc. may be able to help.") Visit the Partnership for Prescription Assistance website (pparx.com) for more information.

I MISSED A DOSE (AND A DOSE AND A DOSE AND ANOTHER DOSE)

For the first couple of years that I took my medication I was diligent about taking the proper dose every single day, just as I was supposed to. Once my psychiatrist asked if I had ever missed a dose, and it seemed like such a silly question—how could I forget to take the medicine that was keeping me well? In the beginning I was desperate to feel better. Forgetting to take a pill would have been like forgetting to drink water in the desert or forgetting to eat after fasting.

I've learned, though, that it is not unusual for people to forget a dose. If this happens to you, contact your doctor for advice on what to do. He or she may tell you to take it when you realize you forgot it, to wait until the next time you are scheduled to take it, or to follow another course of action.

Although I never *forgot* to take my medication, I ran into a pretty scary situation a few years ago when I found myself completely out of money and thus unable to afford my medication (not to mention much else, causing lots of stress and many trips to the mailbox looking for a paycheck).

I've been a freelancer since graduating from college—sometimes I've freelanced exclusively from home; other times I've had a part-time office job as well. While I currently have a full-time job with benefits, I haven't always had insurance or a steady paycheck, which means there have been times I didn't have money for my medication. I have learned that I must—*must*—make my medication a priority over all other purchases, whether they be cookies, shoes, or even milk.

But a couple summers ago I hadn't yet learned that lesson. I was freelancing from home and had to pay for everything health-related out of pocket. I ran out of money for my medication and wasn't able to take it for several days. I began experiencing withdrawal symptoms and left an emotional message for my psychiatrist, after hours, asking for his help. I can't be sure it made any sense. Since I had called his office, not his cell phone, I didn't hear back until the next morning. I had made it through the night and woken up to a voicemail my psychiatrist's nurse had left earlier that morning. Although she encouraged me to call back to discuss my options, I was on a deadline, so I foolishly decided it would be too time-consuming to find a solution.

Instead, I continued pushing my way through the project due that afternoon—making an index for a terribly boring book about trains—and on top of how mind-numbingly dull it was, my hands were shaking and my cheeks were twitching. My brain kept "hiccupping." I was so scared and frustrated I started to cry. So there I was, sitting at my dining room table trying to finish up a project on time, crying with shaky hands and twitchy cheeks. I tried to make the twitching stop by squeezing my cheeks with my hands, but guess what? Didn't work.

In desperation I started up an online chat with a former coworker. I told her how awful I was feeling, all about my withdrawal symptoms, and that I couldn't afford to get my medication. My friend was worried about me and offered to buy my medication for me.

It was kind of a crappy feeling, letting a former coworker bring me to the pharmacy and pay for the medication I should have bought for myself weeks before, but pride seemed a lot less important at that point.

She picked me up and drove me to the pharmacy, where I learned some valuable information I'll pass on to you. The pharmacist told me that in the future I should just let him know about my predicament—sometimes you can get some pills right away, and then you just get fewer pills in the next bottle you buy, making up for those you already got. Or—and this is what I insisted on that day, so my friend didn't have to spend too much money on me—I could buy just a few pills to tide me over.

My friend also bought pizza and sat with me for a few hours that evening. I felt a lot better but was still feeling goofy in my head, so it was great to have company.

There are a few things to note about this friend helping me. One is that she wasn't even a very close friend—lots of people are willing to help, not just your best friends or family members. But I should also point out that we were both adults. She was an experienced adult who knew how to help. Your friends might be willing to help too, which is great. But it's usually better to ask someone who knows a thing or two about it and is even over 18 so the person has more power to help. It's best to ask your doctor for advice on what to do next.

I TOOK TOO MANY PILLS!

Once, I accidentally took two doses within minutes of each other. I was out to dinner with my husband, perusing the menu and chatting away, and I reached into my purse, shook out my usual dose of three pills, and swallowed them with a few gulps of soda. We kept chatting, and I kept flipping through the menu, and again I reached into my purse, shook out three pills, and swallowed them with a few gulps of soda. Then I froze. With bugged-out eyes I said to Peter, "Oh no! I think I just took two doses of Paxil in a row!" I scrambled to grab my purse and anxiously pawed through the contents—hardly necessary since I had just put my pills right back in. I poured them out onto the table and counted. But since I had no idea how many pills were in the bottle before we went to dinner, counting them wasn't very helpful. Peter helped me calm down and assured me I'd be okay until we were through with dinner and I could call my doctor or a pharmacist to make sure I was all right. I had taken 120 milligrams of a mood-altering drug in the span of a few minutes, and that made me very nervous.

After dinner we went to the pharmacy where I have my prescription filled, and the pharmacist's eyes widened when I told him how many milligrams I had taken. He immediately looked up paroxetine to see how I might be affected by doubling my dose, and then explained that it has a short half-life, meaning it wouldn't last too long in my system. (That's why I had those troubling withdrawal symptoms when I missed a few doses.) Other than feeling a little jittery, which could have been due to my panicked reaction, I felt fine.

While my husband ended up being right about telling me to wait, if you accidentally take too many doses, follow this advice instead: Contact your doctor right away. Some medications can make a person very drowsy, so if you take too much you really shouldn't drive or operate other heavy machinery. Also, some medications have a longer half-life than mine does, so if you ever have questions it's important to talk to a professional.

A good strategy is to get a pillbox with separate compartments like you may have seen in your grandparents' medicine cabinet. That way you will know if you've already taken your dose for the day. After this incident I bought a smallish one with seven compartments (a weeks' worth) that fit in my purse, and it helped me keep track. It also gave me a better idea of when I would run out and need a refill. Pouring a dose into my hand wasn't a great way to keep track of how many pills were left in the prescription bottle, but seeing through the clear plastic compartments of my pillbox was. It's also helpful to take your pills at the same time every day, like at breakfast, before you shower, before dinner, or before bed.

One other important note: If you have purposely taken too many pills to hurt yourself, call 911. *But please don't let it get that far.* If you are so low that you are considering suicide or hurting yourself, tell someone immediately. Call a suicide hotline*, a trusted adult, a friend, a parent—do whatever it takes to get someone on the line so you can talk it out with someone. And if you aren't already seeing a therapist, do. People love you even when you find it almost impossible to love yourself, and they want you to get help.

HOW LONG WILL I NEED TO BE ON MEDICINE?

After several years of taking my antidepressant, I talked with my psychiatrist about possibly reducing the dosage. Truth be told, I wanted to know if cutting back from my dose of 60 milligrams a day would help me lose weight. I haven't fully embraced the lifestyle change that would help me drop the pounds I gained after going on paroxetine, and I guess I wanted to see if there might be an easier way out (I know, I know—I need to follow my own advice!). He informed me that lowering my dose would make no difference, explaining that while the drug may lead to weight gain when a

---

*See page 13 for more information.

person starts it, *losing* the weight is not affected by the drug. I said I didn't mind taking medication for the rest of my life if needed, but he assured me I probably wouldn't need to anyway.

There is no conclusive evidence that OCD needs to be treated with lifelong medication. To begin with, not everyone with OCD takes medication. Those who do may take it for six months or so, or for several years, or somewhere in between. If your doctor prescribes medication and thinks you'll need to take it for months, rather than years, he or she may also recommend that you engage in cognitive behavioral therapy to help prevent a relapse of your symptoms once you stop the medication. Remember, never just stop taking your medication. You and your doctor will decide together whether you can stop taking it, and your dose will be gradually lowered until it is out of your system.

On the other hand, you may need to take it for years, like I have. I really am okay with my medication, and I hope you will be, too, if you need to take it. I am more worried that if I go off it my symptoms will come back and I'll feel horrible again. My psychiatrist agreed that this can be a concern, and most doctors would rather keep their patients on antidepressants just in case, since the alternative can be so heartbreaking. Not only that, but once a person goes off a medication that has worked well, it may not have the same effect if the person decides to go back on it. Swallowing a few pills every day is nothing compared to my worst OCD days, and you might feel that way, too. Just keep the lines of communication open and take your doctor's advice to heart.

You may find you need more than just medication. See Chapter 3 for more information about effective therapy and Chapter 5 for other steps you can take to treat your OCD symptoms.

WHAT ELSE HELPS?

"The two most powerful warriors are patience and time."

—Leo Nikolayevich Tolstoy

After seeing the same psychiatrist for several years, I got a letter in the mail. It was from Dr. Grant—he was letting all his patients know he had accepted a position in another state.

I was crushed. Dr. Grant was the first person I had told about the nature of my obsessions, and he treated me with such compassion I couldn't imagine any other psychiatrist taking his place.

But when I thought about it more carefully, I realized that as much as Dr. Grant had done for me in the beginning, our visits had become fewer and farther in between. And we rarely talked about OCD. Rather, we talked about daily work stresses and bigger career decisions, relationship issues and arguments—regular stuff.

Meeting with Dr. Grant reminded me how far I'd come, and just seeing his face made me feel grateful. But I didn't *need* Dr. Grant, not in the way I once had. I had built a great support system that kept me well in my everyday life, and I had learned self-help skills. As much as I would miss Dr. Grant, I would be okay without him.

And as helpful—and at times, critically important—as your therapy sessions may be for you, you can learn self-help techniques, too. You can read books like this one or by therapists who have worked with OCD patients for years. You can build a support system. And if you find that you need *more* than weekly or monthly therapy sessions, there are other options. We are all unique individuals, and that means we will treat our OCD symptoms in different ways. While medication or cognitive behavioral therapy (see page 59) can be very helpful for some people with OCD, other people will need to try other avenues. This chapter covers many of them, from techniques you can try yourself to more intensive options such as long-term care and even brain surgery.

A positive attitude and optimism can go a long way in successfully treating your OCD symptoms. As long as you keep up hope for a better life, you will never stop trying to get better. No matter what you do, whether it's reading self-help books, learning calming techniques, or checking into a long-term treatment program, keep up hope, first and foremost. You have what it takes to manage your OCD symptoms and lead a more carefree life.

SELF-HELP

I've spent a lot of time reading through messages posted to a Facebook OCD support page. I often want to—and often do—chime in with suggestions for how the posters can feel better. So what strategies have worked the best for me?

Reading Books

I am realizing now how many of the little self-help strategies I have been using are from the books I read years ago. There are people who care so much about people like us that they have devoted their entire careers to OCD. Here are a few that have helped me.

- *The Imp of the Mind: Exploring the Silent Epidemic of Obsessive Bad Thoughts* by Lee Baer, Ph.D. This book helped me tremendously, because its primary focus is on the same "bad thoughts" I struggled with for so many years. It's packed with case studies and examples of bad thoughts other people worked hard to overcome.

- *Getting Control: Overcoming Your Obsessions and Compulsions* by Lee Baer, Ph.D. Another book by Baer, but this one isn't specific to any one type of obsession or compulsion. As the subtitle implies, it's a how-to guide on dealing with obsessions and compulsions and contains helpful checklists and coping techniques.

- *Stop Obsessing! How to Overcome Your Obsessions and Compulsions* by Edna B. Foa and Reid Wilson. This practical book has step-by-step programs for overcoming obsessions and compulsions, charts and guides, questionnaires, and tips on how to find a therapist.

Using Self-Calming Techniques

I will still have something pop up in my head and I panic a bit—not again! And I feel afraid. But a little calming self-talk helps. I've combined a few bits of advice into one particularly helpful technique I've used over the years. I read in *Stop Obsessing!* that the first thing I should do when an obsession pops into my head is to accept the thought. Fighting obsessions makes them stronger. From there I think, "That thought isn't helpful right now. Now is not the time to think about it. I can think about it later." And one night my friend Mandi said she likes to imagine putting a stressful thought in a box and closing the lid over it. I combine these two tips and imagine myself putting my obsession away in the box; then I tell myself I can think about it later if I need to; and then I imagine closing the lid and pushing the box away. It might seem a little kooky, but it works really well for me.

You can also calm yourself with deep breathing. Take a long, slow breath in through your nose, imagining your lungs filling with air from the bottom up. Hold the breath for three steady counts, then slowly exhale through your mouth, pursing your lips and relaxing the muscles in your face, jaws, shoulders, and stomach.

Many people get relief from acupressure—applying pressure to specific pressure points on your body that can help you feel better, relieve your stress, or relax you. One such point, called the Third Eye Point, is great for relieving stress and helping you focus. It's located between your eyes, at the top of your nose just below the ridge of your forehead. With firm but gentle pressure, press it with your thumb or the eraser of a pencil for about a minute, making small circles. Do it again 15 minutes later.

Spending Time in Nonjudgmental Settings

Animals don't judge. Neither do little kids (although they are brutally honest). So hang out with your pets—play fetch with your dog or nap with your cat. Play with your younger siblings, cousins, or neighbors. What if your obsessions involve children or animals? Well, then, it's even more important that you spend time with them, but of course it will be different at first, not a pleasant distraction but one of those "forced into therapy" situations. But, really, do what relaxes you most so you can have some moments of peace. Let your family know what you want to do to try to take your mind off of things, and ask that they respect your privacy when you need it.

Staying Busy

The more active you are the less time you'll have to obsess. Sometimes I feel better after doing the dishes—and I often feel motivated to keep moving. Clean your room or living area, take a walk, write a long email to a friend, or go shopping. Of course, it's hard to do when you're in the throes of an obsessive state, so you may need to plan activities you'll feel obligated to do. Join a club, sign up to volunteer, get a part-time job—or do homework! Even making plans with a friend to play one-on-one basketball can ensure you get out of the house and take your mind off your obsessions.

Getting Enough Sleep

This may be old news, but it's worth repeating: You need at least eight hours of sleep a night, and if you're in your teens you need eight and one-half to nine and one-half hours per night. Plan to go to bed at the same time every night and get up the same time every morning, even on weekends. Commit to a nightly ritual, and don't eat, drink, or exercise within a few hours of your bedtime. Research suggests that screen time before bed interferes with sleep, and even the glowing light from your alarm clock or cell phone near your bed could keep you from a full night's sleep. I use my cell phone as my alarm clock, so I turn it upside down and make sure my room is completely dark. I've read that pets can disrupt sleep as well, but I love cuddling with my dog—he keeps me warm, and he wouldn't stand for a change in *his* routine!

Worries and obsessions may keep you up at night, which can have a negative effect on everything that happens the following day. Even though I don't obsess like I used to, I still struggle with racing thoughts while I'm trying to fall asleep. A great strategy for putting those thoughts away for the night is writing everything down on a to-do list that you can focus on *tomorrow*. You can make a list like this even for your icky obsession. The to-do action could be to address it later and to note that now is not the time to be thinking of such things—now is the time for sleeping.

Nighttime isn't the only time to prepare for sleep: daytime actions can help, too. If you exercise during the day, avoid long naps, and generally manage your stress levels, your quality of sleep will benefit.

Exercising

Exercise is great and beneficial for too many reasons to count (but let's try anyway). As I mentioned before, regular exercise can help you sleep at night. It can also help you maintain a healthy weight and help prevent health problems such as stroke, type 2 diabetes, and certain types of cancer.

Regular exercise can also prevent depression. It helps your body release brain chemicals called neurotransmitters and endorphins, which make you feel happier and more relaxed, reduce immune system chemicals that can make depression worse, and increase body temperatures, which can calm you down. Keep in mind that exercise will ease your depression symptoms most effectively if you make it a lifelong habit. That may sound daunting, but it doesn't have to be—walking your dog, riding your bike to school or work, or playing touch football with your friends are all forms of exercise. There's no need to run on a treadmill or lift weights at a gym unless that's what you really want to do. Aim for at least 30 minutes a day, three to five days a week, or break it up into more manageable 15-minute increments.

While exercise is highly recommended to keep you more relaxed and balanced and help relieve depression, don't expect miracles. If you are depressed because of your OCD, exercise on its own can't give you the relief you're looking for. Am I contradicting what I just said and suggesting that you don't exercise? No. But don't *just* exercise. Remember, you need to retrain your brain. Exercise will boost your energy, improve your quality of sleep, and reduce your risk for certain health conditions—all essential for your well-being. Retraining your brain, though, takes support like strategies, therapy, and medication.

Eating Well

Remember "Why Do I Have OCD?" in Chapter 1 on page 29, and the information about neurotransmitters? Well, neurotransmitters can only communicate properly with the help of amino acids, which are found in protein-rich foods, and vitamins B6 and B12. Make sure your diet includes such foods as nuts, fish, whole grains, and lean protein. You can also take dietary supplements, the keyword being *supplement*—vitamins can't replace a nutritious, whole-food diet.

All these self-help options can be great techniques for just that: helping yourself. But none of them alone is a solution to OCD. Life habits like exercising, sleeping and eating well, and staying busy are tools you can use to feel better. They can add to treatment and be a good base for a healthy life, but you still need to do your therapy, take your medicine, and whatever else your doctor or therapist has recommended.

BEYOND BASIC OUTPATIENT THERAPY

Don't lose heart if you participate in therapy routinely (such as monthly, biweekly, or once a week) and you don't see as much progress as you had hoped for. Be sure to let your therapist know if you think counseling isn't helping—perhaps there are other things you could try, or maybe you haven't given your therapist's suggestion a fair chance. If you haven't tried medication yet, you might want to consider it now. There are more intensive options out there, too, and your therapist can help you decide what your next steps should be.

One possibility is **intensive outpatient therapy,** where you would attend several group sessions and one individual session per day, several days per week, at a clinic or other treatment center. You would still live at home, and you would probably have free time between meetings.

If you were to join a **day program,** you would attend treatment for full days at a mental health treatment center, most likely 9:00 a.m. to 5:00 p.m., Monday through Friday. **Partial hospital** treatment is also a day program, but it takes place at a mental health hospital rather than a treatment center. If you need a structured environment but don't need 24-hour supervision, one of these options may be right for you.

Inpatient therapy takes place in a mental health hospital, often in a locked unit. You might choose to join this type of program, or it may be decided for you if you can't care for yourself or you've tried or threatened to harm yourself or others. The goal of inpatient therapy is to stabilize your condition so you can be safely released.

A **residential program** is the highest level of care. In this situation you would live in an unlocked mental health treatment center or hospital, where you would engage in therapy. In addition to therapy, the benefit of living on site is that you can devote your time completely to treating your OCD symptoms in a safe, monitored environment. A residential program is especially helpful if your OCD is severe or you've tried weekly outpatient therapy or a day program but it hasn't been effective.

Rachel's Story: I Got the Help I Needed in a Residential Program

I have mental scars—proof that I have faced insurmountable challenges and have emerged again on the other side. While there is currently no cure for OCD, managing it is possible, but not without complete dedication, because it is grueling work. Overcoming OCD changes you, simple as that. My struggle with OCD has left me with invaluable skills that have served me well in life outside of OCD, but it certainly took a while for me to see that.

I was diagnosed formally with OCD my freshman year of high school. While it was relieving to put a name to the obsessions that had been plaguing my mind and the compulsions that had been hijacking my life for the past year, I had no idea how hard it was going to be to overcome this disorder. I spent my freshman and sophomore years of high school experimenting with different therapies (and therapists) and countless medications to try to take the edge off the anxiety. All the while, I continued to stay actively involved in my academically rigorous high school and on my school and club volleyball teams.

By the end of my sophomore year, I knew my disorder was getting worse despite my efforts to manage it. I realized that in order to properly tackle the disorder, I needed to make it my primary focus. Rather than work, travel, or play—as most of my friends did—during the summer between my sophomore and junior years, I voluntarily hospitalized myself at an inpatient facility in a completely different state. For

over two months I lived in a special unit for teens with OCD
and other anxiety disorders. There, I was able to confront my
illness directly in a collaborative environment surrounded by
people just like me.

I remember begging my mom to go home when we were
on our way there that morning. I have never been good with
separation, and this felt like getting dropped off at overnight
camp all over again. The intake process was long and surreal.
I met with so many people who were asking me a million
questions that I had heard a million times before: *When did
your symptoms start? How do they manifest themselves? Does
anyone in your family have OCD? Are you currently depressed?
Have you ever contemplated suicide? What is your goal here?*

I moved into my bare room, a clone of all the others on the
unit, and tried to make it feel more like the home it would be
for the next several weeks. I had my own twin bed and small
desk that were separated from my roommate's by a small half-
wall. The tiny bathroom was ours to share—something I would
later discover to be an exposure in itself for my germ-obsessed
roommate. Across the hall, another girl was moving in and
we quickly bonded over the fact that our birthdays were only
a day apart. She would soon become my closest friend there
and, I believe, a major reason why I actually *enjoyed* my time
on the unit.

I met the handful of other patients later that evening
at a group meeting. OCD was (and still is) underdiagnosed
in children and young adults, so our unit was very small in
comparison to the adult unit next door. One boy had signs all
over his door with satanic phrases and blasphemous things
written in big black marker; another girl sat far away from
anyone else, terrified to touch anything but her own body;
yet another girl seemed to be chanting something under her
breath the entire meeting. The people I met that night showed
me how functional I truly was in the whole scheme of things.
Before coming, I had felt like I was living two completely
separate lives: one as a fairly successful student who stayed
actively involved with athletics and a social life, and another

behind closed doors and inside my head, where my OCD dictated my every move. At that moment, I knew that if I had not come to the treatment center when I did that I would surely have become as encumbered as my peers were.

Our daily schedule was strictly regimented. Our wake-up call was promptly at 7:15 a.m. (8:00 a.m. on weekends!) if we wanted to have breakfast with the group. The cafeteria was set up buffet style and resulted in many of us gorging ourselves at each meal. The food was less than memorable, but along with learning tools to manage my OCD, I learned of my love for red velvet cake and became an expert at filling a disposable coffee cup with soft-serve chocolate-vanilla swirl after each meal—even breakfast.

After returning from breakfast, we all met in the common area for check-in, where we discussed as a group each of our plans for the day. The rest of the morning consisted of tackling fears on our personal hierarchies in sequential order from the bottom up. While my friends and roommates went off to touch doorknobs of public restrooms and sit in the waiting room of the local AIDS clinic, I drew all over my body with purple marker (an unlucky color) and practiced saying equally unlucky words out loud.

In the afternoons, I attended summer school. Many teens in our unit and the larger neighboring teen unit (whom we referred to as "troubled teens") were at the hospital year-round and had to keep up with their schoolwork. After school we had some free time and often used it to play cards or watch one of the many DVDs on the unit, which usually ended up being either *Zoolander* or *Chicago*. After dinner, we would have CBT (see page 59) where we would learn techniques for decreasing our anxiety levels during exposures as well as ways to combat our negative thoughts. Often times we simply sat in a dark room and had to imagine ourselves relaxing on a beach somewhere. I have never been good at meditation, so I must admit I did not use this time to my advantage, because I was usually thinking about other things.

After a week of "good behavior" (not hard for our rule-following crew), which was tallied on a giant whiteboard in the hallway, our group was allowed to leave the grounds and go on outings to the movies or to dinner. It was strange to be walking around a strip mall with throngs of normal teenagers who had been dropped off by their parents knowing that at the end of the night, I was going to have to leave with the ever-present chaperone and return to a facility where we were checked on every 15 minutes, even during the night.

Our computer and phone time was strictly monitored, too. Once a week I was given a phone to hook up to the telephone jack in my bedroom and was allowed to talk for a half hour. However, I predominately communicated with friends and family via email, which was allowed each night for a short amount of time. As a teenager who was obsessed with instant messaging, this time limit was a huge annoyance. I'm sure today the most difficult thing would be the hospital confiscating all cell phones upon arrival.

I had always planned to leave the unit before school began in the fall, and luckily by that time I had gotten to a place where the doctors were comfortable with my leaving and taking my newfound "skills" to the "real world."

Looking back, I was, and still am, a tough case. My OCD did not manifest itself in a "typical" way (fear of germs, checking, counting, performing lengthy rituals); rather, I was overly concerned with things being lucky or unlucky. There were a few instances that caused me to concretely link something mundane and ordinary to a "bad luck" occurrence, but usually certain things just felt "wrong" so I would go to extremes to avoid or neutralize the triggers. Therefore, my triggers were ever-changing; new things would always be popping up as I navigated daily life—even in such a rigid and controlled environment as we had on the unit. All the while, I knew that I was not there to be *cured* of OCD as much as given the tools to reenter my "normal" life and manage it day to day.

My therapists at home had seldom given me an ounce of ERP (see page 60), and any homework they assigned, I'd put off (much like I did with my regular academic homework). The result was I just hadn't been getting any better. When I left the unit, I still had more work that needed to be done. But my hospitalization marked the first time that I had actually had someone next to me, forcing my hand to do some of those things that caused me such anxiety. Being in a facility and actually practicing exposures 24/7 was the difference between remaining in a paralyzing cycle of anxiety and regaining control of my life.

Everyone on the unit, doctors and patients, taught me to constantly be in tune with myself and reflective as to how I was feeling. These skills are essential for dealing with this condition, but as an unexpected side benefit I became much more introspective and insightful—skills that have proven to be invaluable in life regardless of mental health issues. Thanks to the many coping mechanisms I learned, I am now able to live a more normal and significantly less anxious life. I no longer view my disorder as a burden (well, maybe a little), but rather as a learning opportunity one seldom gets so early in life. I was faced with what seemed like an insurmountable challenge, and after stumbling at the beginning, I met that challenge and moved on with enthusiasm, optimism, and a better understanding of myself.

I am not fully cured of OCD and never will be, but the coping mechanisms I acquired and the insights I gained during my inpatient experience have taught me the meaning of perseverance and have given me a skill set that well positions me to succeed in anything I choose to do in life. These are the "scars" I carry with me, and I'm proud of them.

Rachel was 23 when she wrote this essay.

SURGERY

At my lowest point I recalled a Sunday school teacher I'd had as a child. He had had a lobotomy—an extreme form of brain surgery—and for some reason told us young children about it. Anyway, the idea of having a lobotomy in order to forget my worst thoughts and prevent new ones from popping up was oddly appealing—even if I ended up glassy-eyed and drooling (as I imagined I might), it seemed like a better alternative than being miserable and seeing no light at the end of the tunnel.

The good news is that I got better, and I no longer feel that kind of despair. The great news is that doctors stopped performing lobotomies decades ago (the last one was performed in 1967) and they can now recommend many other treatments that are less controversial and scary. At the time, lobotomies were considered a savior to mentally ill individuals, but science has grown by leaps and bounds. Surgery remains an alternative to traditional therapy and medication if needed, but today's options are less invasive.

Surgery is considered a last resort after you have exhausted all other options. I know that when I was very depressed I felt a measure of hope when I learned that surgery was an option. Try to think of it that way for yourself as well, as a possible future option just in case. You most likely won't need it, but it's out there, so don't give up hope.

All the same, it's really important that you fully participate in whatever you are doing to feel better, because the treatment is most likely to succeed if you are committed to it and believe in its ability to help. Do not give up until you have tried everything. Actually, don't give up then, either.

Though rarely performed and still evolving, the following types of surgery are currently available for patients whose OCD has not responded to medication or therapy. They target the areas of the brain that become hyperactive when an individual's OCD symptoms have been triggered: the orbitofrontal cortex, anterior cingulate cortex, and caudate nucleus, all part of the corticostriatal circuit.

According to the OCD Foundation, about 50 percent of patients who did not respond to behavior therapy or medicine got some benefit from an **anterior cingulotomy.**

About 50 to 60 percent of patients who have undergone an **anterior capsulotomy** after not responding to behavior therapy or medicine got some benefit, and about 60 percent of patients who have undergone a **gamma knife procedure** after not responding to behavior therapy or medication for OCD got some benefit.

Deep brain stimulation (DBS) is a relatively new procedure, but a study found that out of 26 patients with treatment-resistant OCD, 61.5 percent had a positive response to the procedure.

BELIEVE IN YOURSELF

No matter what you're doing to overcome your OCD, or which stage you are in, you should be unbelievably proud of yourself for the effort and progress you are making. Sometimes it feels easier to continue the struggle on your own and not talk about what you're going through, but the more support you have, the better. And please know this: Even though you may have days or weeks or months when you feel that you are unworthy of support or believe that no one in this world could possibly understand what you are going through, that's just not true.

You *are* worthy. You are worthy of every hug, pat on the back, encouraging smile, compliment, therapy session, pill, doctor, friend, and family member. And you are worthy of a brighter future in which you will have moments when you are not just depressed, not just scared or fearful, not just ashamed or upset or obsessive, but ecstatically happy, blue, frustrated, *meh*, stressed, so-so, pretty happy—the whole range of emotions everyone should be experiencing throughout life.

CHAPTER 6

I AM NOT OCD: POPULAR PERCEPTIONS AND STIGMAS

"I couldn't go up to my mom and say,
'You know, there's things going on in
my head you don't even wanna know.'
I would never do that. I wouldn't tell
my friends, I wouldn't tell a teacher."

—Howie Mandel

There was a time when I didn't understand depression; in fact, I feared it, not as a condition that could or would befall me, but as a condition in others. In college I had an enormous crush on a guy until I found out he had a history of clinical depression. I'm ashamed to admit it now, but I didn't think I could deal with something like that. I think I thought depression was the same thing as insanity; I'm not exactly sure what perceptions I had as an 18-year-old, but I do know I was uninformed and judgmental. It is very important to me that other people are informed and that the stigma that surrounds mental illness in general, and depression in particular, is quashed.

I think I first began to understand and sympathize with depression when I seriously dated a young man who had been dealing with depression his whole life. We dated for three years, and although I, too, struggled with depression during that time, I always put his mental well-being first. I never admitted to myself or anyone else how I felt, and for some reason I believed that however low I felt it couldn't possibly be classified as depression. It wasn't that I didn't want help, it was just that I thought whatever I was going through couldn't possibly compare with what *truly* depressed people went through. I never took the time to analyze my own feelings or what I needed; my boyfriend went through so many ups and downs that I was constantly worried about him. I never even mentioned to him how I was feeling, even though there were nights I cried myself to sleep.

I put all of my energy toward helping him; the problem was that he wasn't at all willing to help himself. He went off his anti-depressants and refused to go back on them or any other kind of antidepressant, and he also refused to talk to a therapist because he was afraid he'd be locked up in a psychiatric ward. During the three years we dated he struggled through depressive periods without ever seeking help for himself. I finally realized there was nothing I could do to help him, nothing I could do to make him happy.

I think having had such a close relationship with a depressed person actually helped me when I finally realized I was depressed myself. I was surprisingly afraid to admit I needed antidepressants; it felt like such a huge step, but somehow being with that boyfriend made me realize that it was okay to need medication. I had always told him there was nothing wrong with needing antidepressants, that taking them to feel better was no different than a person with diabetes using insulin, but he foolishly let the cruel stigma surrounding mental illness keep him from seeking the help he needed. I had said it to him so many times I had to believe it for myself when the time came.

Molly's Story: Stigma Made OCD Feel Worse

I started having obsessive-compulsive tendencies when I was about 15, and was diagnosed when I was 16. When I was 14 I was molested by a family member, and that is what more than likely triggered my OCD. I never told anybody about my molestation, so I bottled everything up inside, which made me more stressed out and ultimately made my OCD worse.

Stress is what I think influences OCD the most. Some people might disagree, but I know that my worst days with this disorder are usually days when I am stressed out about something. I have days where I just want to lie in bed all day because I know when I step foot on the floor the struggle begins. I used to be angry, asking myself why God would let me have this disorder. I went through a period where all I did was drink, smoke weed, and self-harm until I realized I couldn't let OCD define who I am.

There are many stereotypes about OCD, one of them being that we are faking or causing it ourselves. My parents never understood this disorder and always thought it was in my head, and I used to be really angry with them for not being supportive. But now I understand that this is a very hard disorder to grasp. I never had the support of parents or family while battling OCD, and am just now getting a little bit of "support" by my mom.

Growing up, I lived in a relatively small town, so everybody knew your business whether you wanted them to or not. I was too scared to get help because I thought someone would find out and look at me differently if they knew I had OCD. Once I started college, I found a therapist and started getting counseling for my OCD. Looking back now, I wish I had gotten counseling sooner because it has helped me tremendously and it might have saved me from some of the mistakes I made as I was trying to figure out how to deal with OCD.

I am now 19 years old and still struggle with OCD daily, but it is way better controlled than when I was younger because I finally got help. Counseling hasn't "fixed" me, but it has made it better for me by giving me healthy coping methods to aid in the fight against OCD. I remember the numerous times I wanted to give up, just call it quits. I attempted to end my life twice, but thank God I am still here. I will more than likely struggle with OCD for the rest of my life, and somehow I am now okay with that.

I try not to let this disorder rule my life, as it once did. I am definitely not saying that I still don't have those days where I don't want to get out of bed, but now I am way more optimistic about my future, and counseling helped me tremendously. I am now a full-time college student and have a part-time job. If I knew when I was 15 years old what I know now, my entire life would have been different, and I think about that every day. If I would have gotten help earlier, reached out to another family member, a teacher, or a friend, I wouldn't have gone through the negative ways of trying to cope with this disorder. But then again, all of the things I have been through in my life have made me a better person, and have shaped me into the strong person I am today.

Molly was 19 when she wrote this essay.

Awareness of mental illness—whether it's depression, OCD, or another disorder—is key, and it's partly why I talk about my OCD. It is why I "talk" to perfect strangers on Facebook to reassure them they're not alone. It's why I wrote this book and why, despite social anxiety and a public-speaking phobia, I will even speak about it to others.

EVERYONE AND THEIR BROTHER THINK THEY HAVE OCD

As with depression, not many people understand all aspects of OCD. I don't blame them; I didn't know much about it until I suspected I had the disorder myself. People tend to associate OCD with very visible symptoms and kooky television or movie characters. Melvin Udall, Jack Nicholson's character in the movie *As Good as It Gets,* has obsessive-compulsive disorder, and he performs such stereotypical rituals as stepping around cracks in the sidewalk. The main character on the old TV series *Monk* has a grave fear of germs, so he washes his hands incessantly and wears gloves while solving crimes. He is also afraid of the dark, heights, and milk.

People love to refer to themselves as "OCD" as though it's a charming trait. "I'm so OCD!" they'll say with a laugh after they've straightened some papers on their desk or rubbed sanitizer into their hands during cold and flu season. I used to do the same from time to time—turns out, I *do* have OCD, but I'm still not sure if the "symptoms" I joked about in the past are actual indications of the disorder.

Is joking about a mental disorder as bad as using a racial slur? Not exactly, but it does minimize the disorder and perpetuate stigmas related to it. What we are going through is very painful. "OCD" stands for obsessive-compulsive *disorder*. It is a disorder, not a personality quirk or something that comes out now and then and can be easily laughed about.

I'm not sure what it is that makes people think OCD is no biggie; when was the last time you heard someone say that they're "so psychotic" or "so schizophrenic" and expect you to think it's cool or funny instead of a cause for care and concern? Then again, misconceptions abound when it comes to mental illness in general. I still hear people confuse schizophrenia with multiple personality disorder, and there isn't always a whole lot of compassion for people who experience psychosis.

Even medical professionals who should know better joke about OCD. One week I came down with a very painful stomachache, unlike any I'd ever had before. The emergency room doctor referred me to a gastroenterologist. As I discussed my symptoms and general history with this specialist, I explained to him that my (very different) years-long stomach problems had improved significantly since I had gone on paroxetine.

"Why did you go on that medication?" he asked.

"For depression," I answered, and then hesitated a bit. "Also, I have OCD." It felt like a huge confession, something one shouldn't just blurt out, even to a medical professional.

"Don't we all?" he said with a note of disgust in his voice. "Psychiatry—that's like the designer profession to have. Someone comes to you and says, 'I wash my hands a lot,' and you diagnose them with OCD. It's so easy. By those symptoms everyone in this office has the disorder."

I couldn't believe what I was hearing. This man was actually telling me I had a silly, overdiagnosed disorder. Hey, buddy, you're *supposed* to wash your hands a lot when you work with patients all day.

"Well, that's not me," was all I could say. I took the medication samples he gave me, which did relieve some of my stomach pain, but I never went back to see him again.

In the interest of reducing stigma and furthering acceptance and understanding of OCD, I probably should have politely informed him that while his views are indeed held by others, they represent a misconception. Your mother may tell you it's not polite to correct someone, and in some cases she's probably right, but allowing misconceptions to be perpetuated doesn't help our cause. We can politely tell people they are misinformed, pull them aside to talk to them privately, or use humor to let a person know he's made a faux pas without making the situation super awkward.

It's not always easy to do, though, and we can't always win over skeptics. If you run into people like this, decide whether you find it worthwhile to get the facts straight, and don't let them get you down or discourage you. What you are feeling is real, and someone's rude comment doesn't change that. If your doctor says things like this, you may want to ask for a different doctor.

And according to my psychiatrist, some physicians misdiagnose their patients who report what seem to be symptoms of OCD, and these patients are often referred to him.

"I have to tell them, 'You're a neat freak. You don't have OCD,'" he told me. As strange as it may seem, I was pleased when he shared that with me; I felt assured that my problem is real and that there is someone who understands what I have gone through. I have cried uncontrollably on my couch because I couldn't get a thought out of my head. I have scratched and pinched my cheeks, dug my fingernails into the flesh, because I hoped the physical pain would distract me from the emotional pain a disturbing image was causing me. This mental disorder is more serious than wanting a dust-free bookshelf. OCD is serious for people whose symptoms *do* include fear of germs or whose compulsions include cleaning, but having obsessive-compulsive disorder isn't the same as liking a clean house or an organized desk.

Shortly after my first appointment with Dr. Grant, I spent a Saturday afternoon with my friend Joe. As we were taking a drive around one of Minneapolis' many lakes, I told him how I had been feeling lately and that I had been diagnosed with OCD. I was surprised when he didn't believe it. It wasn't that he was just taken off guard; he thought I had been misdiagnosed because I didn't fit into the symptoms he was most familiar with.

"Are you sure?" he asked. "I've been to your apartment. I mean, it wasn't messy or anything, but it didn't seem like you clean compulsively."

I explained to him that an obsession with germs is only one symptom of OCD and that I mostly just have obsessive thoughts without trying to get rid of them with a corresponding compulsive behavior. (I have since realized that avoiding situations that trigger or make me face the source of my obsessions *is* a compulsion.) I tried to express to him how my irrational fears can completely take over until I feel like I have no control over my own thoughts or happiness.

"Okay," he said, "give me an example of one of these obsessions you're talking about."

"Well . . ."

I hesitated a bit. No one, not even my psychiatrist, knew the specifics of my deepest fears. Dr. Grant knew in general what I had been struggling with, but he knew how painful it would be for me to detail any of my obsessions with him. He knew enough to comfort me and let me know I wasn't alone.

I chose a "safe" example to share with Joe.

"When I was little, I had a fear of being burned alive. And it wasn't just that I was afraid it *might* happen; I was sure it was going to happen. I would cry in bed at night and ask God why I had to be in a fire. I worried about it constantly."

"Huh," he said. I think he sympathized with me, but because what he knew about OCD didn't match up with what he knew about me, he didn't seem convinced.

WHAT OCD IS *NOT*

OCD is not a collection of cute or quirky personality traits. It's not limited to obvious compulsions like excessive washing, avoiding cracks in the sidewalk, or checking to make sure the door is locked. It is different things to different people, something many people don't understand. Your OCD symptoms may not be anything like mine, and mine may not be anything like the next person's.

There have been a few times when I've heard that a celebrity has OCD, but when I look further into it I realize she said offhandedly during an interview that she needs her books to be facing a certain way or something like that. I read an article in which *American Idol* alum Carrie Underwood said she is "OCD about time." Maybe these celebrities really do have OCD and threw just one example out there, or maybe they don't understand OCD and don't realize it's a serious disorder that should be diagnosed by a doctor.

That's why it was so refreshing to learn that when Lena Dunham's *Girls* character, Hannah, exhibited symptoms of OCD in a TV episode, it was actually based on Lena Dunham's own teenage experience with OCD. Not only did the episode show a more serious side of OCD than many shows do, but Dunham also spoke out about her struggles and recommended the International OCD Foundation to her Twitter followers.

Howie Mandel, long-time comedian and currently one of the three hosts on *America's Got Talent,* has OCD and has recently been vocal about his experience with it. During an interview with Larry King,* Mandel had to push a little to make sure King had an accurate understanding of the disorder. Even though Mandel had discussed his OCD with King before, King said, "It's not a severe mental illness. It's not depression."

"I have that," Mandel said immediately. "I wasn't kidding when I said I was medicated. Sometimes it's severe. You know, and some-times it's not. I'm functioning and you know, if I could be on my little soapbox and help remove the stigma of mental health, if you had a bad limb or had something somebody could identify as a physical issue, they'd have no problem with it, and I think it's as severe and debilitating."

Over the years Mandel has joked around about OCD, telling funny stories on nighttime talk shows and making light of his germ phobia. But he's confessed that he joked to mask the pain OCD caused, and when he wrote an honest book about it *(Here's the Deal: Don't Touch Me)* he admitted he felt nervous about sharing the truth. Mandel has done a lot to raise awareness of OCD, something he's accomplished with both candor and humor.

USING HUMOR AS A COPING METHOD

Howie Mandel is a professional comedian, but guess what? You can joke around about OCD, too. It's okay to laugh at yourself, make light of your disorder around others, and have a sense of humor about your condition. In fact, it's normal and healthy to do these

---

*"Howie Mandel on Living with OCD," *Larry King Now,* December 10, 2012.

things, and humor is well known as a great coping device—just be sure not to perpetuate stereotypes, laugh at others, or make fun of OCD without outing yourself to others first.

Be sure you know your audience. If someone doesn't know you have OCD, you run the risk of coming across as insensitive, as though you think it's okay to make fun of someone with a mental disorder. Even if others know you have OCD, it's not enough to brush off jokes with a comment such as, "It's okay, I have OCD."

Laughing about your OCD or poking fun at yourself around your best friend or your family members is one thing, but making broad statements in the presence of others who don't know you well is another. Maybe *you* are okay with joking about your disorder, but it doesn't mean everyone who has OCD is, too. Maybe *you* cope well by poking fun at your obsession or compulsion, but it doesn't mean other people with OCD cope the same way.

Let's say you're in a group (meeting, classroom, party) and you joke about OCD. If not every single person in the room knows you have OCD, they won't know you are making light of your own disorder and day-to-day life. Perhaps someone at the other end of the table has OCD, has generalized anxiety disorder (GAD), has been severely depressed, has a close friend with a mental condition, has family members with a mental condition, and so on. If so, there's a good chance you're offending that person. You come off sounding pretty insensitive.

If you are in group therapy or on a message board, it might be helpful to tell others up front that you use humor as a coping mechanism. Or instead of making a bold statement such as "I'm crazy" or "I'm weird," qualify your statements with "Sometimes when I can't stop my counting rituals I feel so crazy, like maybe I'm insane." That way you are opening your feelings to discussion and comments such as "Me too" or "But you're not—you're not alone."

TIMES HAVE CHANGED

Thankfully for us, doctors and researchers have learned a lot about OCD—and they're still learning. I hope by now I've convinced you that you aren't the only person in the world who has OCD. Lots of other people are dealing with obsessions and compulsions as you read this, and researchers are still learning more about it.

Today there is a name for what you are going through and you have many options for treatment. But imagine if you were Margery Kempe, an Englishwoman born in 1373, who told a clergyman about her obsessive thoughts, now documented in *The Book of Margery Kempe*. She had "many evil thoughts . . . horrible sights and cursed memories. . . . Wherever she went, or whatever she did, these cursed memories remained with her."

What would you tell Margery if you could speak with her now? Would you tell her she wasn't alone, or give her advice on how to feel better?

And then there is Hannah Allen, a 17th-century Englishwoman with OCD, who said, "I was persuaded I had sinned the unpardonable sin. . . . I would often in my thoughts wish I might change conditions with the vilest persons I could think of, concluding there was hopes for them though not for me."

It seems that OCD was so prevalent 300 years ago that John Moore's pamphlet about a "disorder of mind" that caused "unwanted 'naughty' thoughts" had seven editions printed between 1692 and 1708. Moore, a pastor who also preached about this disorder, advised that "when you find these thoughts creeping upon you, be not mightily dejected. . . . Neither violently struggle with them; since experience doth teach that they increase and swell by vehement opposition; but dissipate and waste away, and come to nothing when they are neglected, and we do not much concern ourselves about them."*

How wise. There wasn't proper medication then, but I take comfort in knowing that people with unwanted thoughts had good advice at their disposal. As time goes on, I hope others will realize they have OCD much sooner than many people do, and will get help so they can move on with their lives in as much a "normal" state as possible. OCD is nothing new, but that means we have centuries of anecdotes and research behind us so we can keep moving forward.

---

*Moore, John. *Of Religious Melancholy: A Sermon Preach'd before the Queen at White-Hall, March the 6th, 1691/2* (London: Printed for William Rogers, 1692), pp. 19–27.

OCD AND RELATED DISORDERS

Sometimes OCD can be confused with other disorders, and sometimes people mistake OCD for other disorders because they have symptoms in common. Be as thorough as you can when you share your symptoms with your doctor, even if it's embarrassing to share. You may have OCD and another disorder, and that's okay. The more your doctor understands at the outset, the better equipped she or he will be to get you the right treatment for *you.*

Here is a chart detailing the differences between and similarities to other disorders.*

TOURETTE'S SYNDROME AND TIC DISORDERS

Tourette's syndrome is a mental and nervous system disorder that involves multiple motor and vocal tics that last for more than a year. The tics are largely involuntary.

People with Tourette's syndrome or tic disorders and people with OCD both:

- Repeat physical behaviors like eye blinking, touching, or tapping
- Repeat vocal behaviors like clearing their throat

People with Tourette's syndrome or tic disorders:

- Do their tics because they have a sense of discomfort or need to feel "just right"
- Respond better to habit reversal and to different medicines than people with OCD

People with OCD:

- Do their repetitive behaviors in response to an obsession (thought or image)

TRICHOTILLOMANIA

Trichotillomania is also known as compulsive hair pulling, a response to stressors and fears.

People with trichotillomania and people with OCD both:

- Do repetitive behaviors
- Do repetitive behaviors in response to feeling uncomfortable

People with trichotillomania:

- Get a good feeling from pulling out their body hair; some use it to relieve stress
- Respond better to habit reversal and to different medicines than people with OCD

People with OCD:

- Repeat their behaviors to get away from bad feelings, like anxiety

BODY DYSMORPHIC DISORDER (BDD)

A person who has BDD is preoccupied with an imagined or slight flaw. BDD can cause a person to undergo frequent cosmetic procedures, groom excessively, or avoid social situations.

People with BDD and people with OCD both:

- Do repetitive checking

People with BDD:

- Have checking behaviors and obsessions that only focus on their body or the way they look
- Are very likely to seek cosmetic surgery

People with OCD:

- Do not usually have thoughts or behaviors that focus on the way they look

OBSESSIVE-COMPULSIVE PERSONALITY DISORDER (OCPD)

OCPD is a personality disorder that includes rigid adherence to rules and regulations, an overwhelming need for order, an unwillingness to yield or give responsibilities to others, and a sense of righteousness about the way things "should be done."

People with OCPD and people with OCD both have problems with:

- Making excessive lists
- Perfectionism
- Hoarding

People with OCPD:
- Have problems finishing tasks because of their preoccupation with perfectionism
- Don't see a problem with their symptoms

People with OCD:
- Do not always have perfectionism problems
- Do not like their OCD symptoms

ASPERGER'S DISORDER AND AUTISM

Asperger's disorder and autism are both on the autism spectrum and are developmental disorders that appear in early childhood. Both disorders affect a person's ability to communicate and interact with others.

People with Asperger's disorder or autism and people with OCD both may have:
- "Stereotyped" behaviors like following rigid routines
- An "obsessive" interest in something

People with Asperger's disorder or autism:
- Usually have thoughts and behaviors that focus only on repeating things
- Don't try to prevent their thoughts
- Have severe problems with social interactions

People with OCD:
- Usually have thoughts and behaviors that focus on contamination, violent or sexual themes, checking, etc.
- Try to stop their bad thoughts from happening

IMPULSE CONTROL DISORDERS

Impulse control disorders include addictions to gambling, sexual activity, and excessive shopping or stealing.

People with impulse control disorders and people with OCD both may have:
- Strong urges to repeat certain behaviors
- Attention problems

People with impulse control disorders:
- Repeat their behaviors as a way to increase good feelings like arousal or excitement

People with OCD:
- Repeat their behaviors to get away from bad feelings, like anxiety

PSYCHOTIC DISORDERS

The two major symptoms of psychotic disorders are hallucinations and delusions. People with a psychotic disorder may hear voices other people don't hear, may not make sense when they talk, or engage in strange or dangerous behavior.

People with psychotic disorders and people with OCD both may have:
- Strange or bizarre thoughts
- Thoughts that include sexual, violent, or religious themes

People with psychotic disorders:
- Have delusions; their thoughts aren't based in reality, but they believe the thoughts to be true

People with OCD:
- Usually know that their obsessive thoughts don't make sense, even if they respond to them as though they are "true"
- Can stay in touch with reality in all other areas of their lives

---

I've found that a common misconception about my own OCD is that my small, obvious quirks comprise my disorder. There are so many little things that annoy me or preoccupy me, but I wouldn't say they are symptoms of my OCD. I consider my OCD symptoms to be the very worst of them—the persistent, unwanted, fear-based images. I can live with the little things.

For example, when the clip of a pen cap isn't exactly aligned with the wording on the shaft of the pen, I get very bothered. I always fix the pen cap, whenever the problem arises, wherever the offending pen happens to be—at the bank, in the grocery store, on my desk, on a coworker's desk. In meetings I watch people tap their pens on the conference room table, twirl them in their fingers, chew on the cap, take the cap off, put the cap on, push, pull, push, pull, and I want to reach across the table, grab the pen from their hand, twist the clip into alignment with the brand name, and hand it back. But that would be weird. It would appear crazy. Everyone would say, "Whoa, are you OCD or what?" and laugh. And I would have to laugh along with them and be teased thereafter about that day that I was totally OCD and reached across the table and grabbed the pen from Linda while Amy was talking about the brochure Jack's been designing.

Oh, and if I walk into a kitchen, any kitchen, and a cabinet door or drawer isn't closed, I have to close it. If something is crooked, I have to straighten it.

I don't know if these small annoyances will ever go away, and I'll be blunt: I don't really care if they do or not.

My husband and I adopted a dog several years ago, when the dog, Tuffy, was one year and three months old. Tuffy had been abused and was terrified of men and other dogs. If a man spoke to him, Tuffy would pee on the spot, wherever he was. While Tuffy and I bonded immediately, Peter had to prove he was trustworthy. For weeks Tuffy hid behind my legs when Peter was around. He barked every time Peter walked into a room, and if he *had* to get past Peter he would do what I dubbed his army crawl, frantically scurrying around him. He tried to attack my brothers' dogs. He tore our back door to shreds so we didn't get our deposit back when we moved out. He peed on our bed *and* our guest bed. And once, when we were out and the bedroom door closed behind him with the light off, he panicked so much that he peed, pooped, scratched at the door, and tore up the carpet until he got down to the tacks—which cut him, so he got blood on the walls, carpet, and door as he continued to try to dig his way out.

What's my point? Tuffy has come so incredibly far since his first several months with us that the small behavior problems he still has don't bother us. He still growls and lunges at other dogs on walks, and my parents and brothers wish he didn't jump up on them when they enter our house. I know many a responsible dog owner would work harder to break him of this habit, but we had to put in so much work just to get him to reasonably acceptable behavior that I am okay with some of his remaining not-so-perfect tendencies. And that's how I feel about my pen cap quirk, cabinet door closing, and picture straightening, and even my somewhat irrational worries about my husband's well-being when he doesn't answer his phone.

I don't expect perfection out of my dog or myself. And you don't need to expect perfection out of yourself either.

CHAPTER 7
BEING YOU WITH OCD

"The best way out is always through."

—Robert Frost

I once thought, especially during the depths of my despair, that I would never fully recover from my obsessions. I figured that even if I were able to stop them someday, I would still have the memories of them burned into my psyche where they would be a constant and very unpleasant reminder of what I had once been through. Could I ever truly forgive myself for my thoughts? I didn't know at that time that I didn't have to forgive myself for anything, because what I was going through is part of a disorder that I didn't ask for or deserve, just as someone with cancer needn't forgive himself or herself for being ill. I was in a place of little hope, and even when I thought I could get better I would have a nagging feeling that the reminders of my obsessions would always hurt me.

Have you ever felt that way?

After several years of being on medication and having a great psychiatrist, and after having read books and articles that have helped me realize I am not alone and using cognitive behavioral tools to help me obsess less and fret less when I do, I don't *love* remembering what I have obsessed about over the years, but it doesn't crush me like I once thought it might.

Now that I have been diagnosed, gotten the help I needed, and built a more normal life, I have figured out how to be me—the person I was meant to be. If you haven't done this yet, you will.

PUTTING YOURSELF IN CONTROL

"How can you diagnose someone with an obsessive-compulsive disorder, then act like I have some choice about barging in here?"

—Melvin Udall, Jack Nicholson's character in *As Good as It Gets*, after interrupting his doctor's session with another patient

I liken it to having been afraid of or disturbed by something in childhood. For example, when I was little my mom brought my brothers and me to see *E.T. the Extra-Terrestrial* in the theater. I was absolutely terrified when E.T. got sick toward the end of the movie, and I bawled loudly and uncontrollably. My mom now says she was mortified. For a long time after that, when we would watch *E.T.* as a family, I would be reminded of that scene and make sure I didn't watch it when it came on again. It was still powerful to me.

But now that I'm an adult, it's different. While the memory of poor E.T. being so terribly sick and helpless doesn't mean *nothing* to me anymore, it doesn't upset me the way it used to. At 34 years old, I might be able to watch the whole movie now and be okay with watching that scene. The difference is that when I was young I was vulnerable, innocent, and confused. The first time I saw *E.T.*, I had no idea that sad scene would appear on the big screen. I was struck by it and I couldn't control my emotions, couldn't hide my eyes fast enough, and couldn't let it go for a while afterward. The subsequent times I knew that it was just a movie, that E.T. wasn't real, and I could remind myself that it all turns out in the end.

Let's draw the parallels. When I was in the throes of OCD and depression, I was also vulnerable, innocent, and confused. My obsessions terrified me, and at times they made me cry uncontrollably. I can look back on it now and feel sympathy for myself knowing how unfair and unwanted it all was and how there was nothing I could have done to stop it from happening, at least at first. Before I knew I had OCD and knew I could get help, knew others experienced what I had experienced, and knew how to cope with it on a moment-by-moment basis, I was struck by it and couldn't control my emotions. I didn't see the obsessions coming, and they disturbed me. And I *definitely* couldn't let it all go.

But now I know that I might obsess about something, and I might be scared. I might be very scared. But I also know that I can stop and think for a moment, and say, "It's okay, it will pass. And thinking that thought doesn't mean anything. It's just a thought." I can move on. I can set the thought aside for later and I can usually refrain from judging myself too harshly. Metaphorically speaking (I was an English major, and all English majors have to speak metaphorically now and then), I don't have to replay the scene of E.T. lying helpless on a stainless steel table over and over and over again. I know it will be okay in the end. E.T. goes home. In the same way, I know my obsessions aren't real, and I can have more control over them than they have over me. The trick is to give them less power. They do not define me. I am a good person even if bad thoughts pop into my head.

And I can see my past obsessions for what they were—terrifying scenes in my life that brought me down, made me sad, and made me afraid. Instead of hating myself for what I was once tortured by, I try to feel happy about how far I've come since then. Hey, I once thought I would never be happy again! I didn't know if I could ever sleep alone again, or fall asleep without being in front of the TV. Or if I could get through a day without crying. Those might be givens for people who are not depressed and do not have OCD, but for me they are huge.

Maybe you think you could never leave home without checking the stove over and over again, or maybe you can't imagine not being afraid of germs. But there is hope, and recovery doesn't happen all at once.

BUILDING A COMMUNITY OF SUPPORT

"Don't make friends who are comfortable to be with. Make friends who will force you to lever yourself up."

—Thomas J. Watson

One of the best—and most enjoyable—ways to feel better and make progress toward recovery is to actively engage with your loved ones. I recommend telling your closest friends and family members about your diagnosis.

When I look back on my emails to Mandi (see page 36), I know I was putting on a happy face and faking it even as I was reaching out and asking for help. I denied her the full information and pretended to be better than I was. I know the truth when I read those old emails. We can be very good at pretending to be happier than we really are, and while it's okay to be discreet and not tell every person you run across how miserable you are or what your OCD is like, it's important to tell the *right* people that you are feeling low, bad, horrible, depressed—whatever. Tell people you trust. Keep in mind that "trust" in this type of situation doesn't always mean the same thing as it does in other areas of your life—telling your best friend you are suicidal does not (and should not) mean that your friend will keep it to herself. It means you can trust her not to judge you and that you can trust her to help you.

I know you don't want to worry anyone or make yourself an outcast, but people who care about you will probably worry less if they are well informed about what you're going through. It can be very tempting to withdraw and put on a happy face in order to please others, but you aren't doing anyone, especially yourself, any favors when you do so. If you really believe that certain people in your life will make you feel worse because they are too old-school or stubborn to understand, then don't tell those people—find someone else to tell.

What I have found since being diagnosed with OCD is that most people are interested in learning more about it. At times I have shyly confessed to an old friend or a relative that I have OCD, and I have always been pleasantly surprised at the response I get. I waited a long time to tell my cousin because she follows a much different religion than I grew up with, and I thought she might object to my taking antidepressants. I couldn't have been more wrong. She felt bad that I had been going through it without her knowing, and after our face-to-face conversation she sent me a card telling me how she wished she had known earlier so she could support me and let me know how much she loved me.

I told my mom about the card my cousin had sent and restated what she had written in it—that she felt bad she hadn't known before. My mom didn't speak; her face crumpled a bit, and she looked away from me, pointing to her chest and nodding.

"You wish you had known before too?" I asked her.

She nodded.

She felt like an inattentive mother who hadn't noticed how awful her own child was feeling, but it wasn't her fault. I'm an adult who doesn't live at home anymore (we don't even live in the same city anymore), and I'd worked very hard at hiding what was going on. In truth, though, my mom *did* notice something was up. She could tell I was very sad, but if I didn't tell her why, how could she ever know exactly how to support me?

No person should have to feel alone in their lives, in their struggles, or in their joys. But some people don't understand OCD, accept it, or think that those of us who have it are the normal, interesting, and caring people we really are. Sometimes people say things that are downright mean; they might call someone names like "crazy" or "freak" and might think we aren't as good as them because we have a disorder. Some people don't believe in OCD or depression or mental illness in general.

If there are people in your life who won't treat you as well if they know your secret, then don't tell them. You'll feel so much better about your disorder and yourself if only the people closest to you know about it, because they have enough empathy and understanding to treat you well, listen closely, and respond in helpful ways.

But you might feel that you shouldn't have to hide any part of yourself, and you may feel pride in your disorder because it is part of who you are. That is great! Shout it from the mountaintops, educate the misinformed, the underinformed, and the ignorant, and embrace every single part of you. But you'll probably want to wait to do this until the right time and place. You know, maybe not at your 10-year high school reunion: "What have *I* been up to? Well, I have a mental disorder! I tend to wash my hands upwards of 50 times a day—yep, that's why I insisted on a fist bump—and . . ."

What is the right time and place? While it's a personal decision and different for everyone, it's probably best to tell others when you are relatively comfortable with your diagnosis. Of course, when you tell the first few people it will still be relatively new to you, too. As with most things in life, practice and repetition will make it easier. I didn't tell *everybody* until after I found out this book would be published. If I told people I had a book coming out, they inevitably wanted to know what it was about, and the easiest way to explain was to begin with "I have OCD."

If you think someone you tell will find your news upsetting—maybe a parent—make sure you have time to sit down and answer any questions he or she might have. It might also be a good idea to have some privacy so you feel as comfortable as possible sharing details you might consider embarrassing.

Once you've thought it through a bit, go ahead and tell the important people you've decided to share this with. Just be aware that you won't always be met with enthusiasm or empathy. Tell someone about your disorder when you think you can handle a less-than-sensitive response. And remember that there are many great support groups out there, full of people who understand what you're dealing with (go here for more information).

OCD AND DATING

Part of living a normal life with OCD is having a social life. You don't have to tell everyone you meet casually about your OCD, and you probably shouldn't. But if you begin to date someone, it's probably best to let that person know sooner rather than later because it *could* affect your relationship, especially if you are still really struggling.

I actually started dating my husband a few months before I entered the final obsessive, depressive period that led me to seeing a psychiatrist, which means that he was not only with me through a terrible time in my life, he stuck with me before he *had* to. We were just dating—not living together, not engaged, not married. So if you think your OCD symptoms will keep you from healthy friendships or meaningful relationships, well—think again. It is possible to have OCD and a full, happy life.

Of course, there were times in the early stages of my relationship with Peter that I felt he deserved better than a depressed, anxious, God-knows-what-was-wrong-with-me person, and it *is* hard to start or maintain any relationship when you are not doing well. If you are already dating someone, give the person a chance to be supportive. But if you are going through a rough time or starting a new treatment regimen, you might want to hold off on actively seeking a relationship. When things are intense for you, and you're going toe-to-toe with your OCD, it's important that you put yourself first, because that is what gives you the best chance to get better. It will also give any relationship you enter a fighting chance. It's hard to be happy when you aren't happy. Deep, right? Being depressed or struggling through an obsessive period will make it difficult to commit yourself to another person.

Obviously Peter and I stayed together, and I know how much I can trust him and how much he really loves me because I'm not always the easiest person to live with. If you are already in a relationship, be as honest as you need to be for your boyfriend or girlfriend to understand what you are going through, how available you can be while you get better, and what he or she can do to help. Acknowledge that you need to focus on yourself for a while and that it may be hard for your boyfriend or girlfriend to be patient, but that it is the best for both of you.

OCD AND SCHOOL (AND WORK)

OCD can help in my profession, but it has hindered me as well. I have the patience needed to proofread really carefully and slowly, paying close attention to each word, even each letter and character. On the flip side, I have sometimes read the same sentence over and over (and over) again without making any progress or feeling like I can safely move on to the next sentence, especially when my OCD symptoms were giving me trouble. I just couldn't convince myself that the sentence was fine.

Having this disorder can make everything work-related more difficult—meeting deadlines, doing well on projects, getting everything just right—and if you're still in school you might find it becomes a burden in much the same way.

In kindergarten I always colored dark by pressing down really hard—I had to have my pictures *just so*—and one day my teacher wouldn't let me go to recess until I finished my picture with lighter coloring. In junior high I was always behind in homework, even "fun" art projects. I was too meticulous. Everyone else would be making Rudolph the Red-Nosed Reindeer while I was still working on a Thanksgiving turkey. In high school I would get so behind in my homework that I'd be failing, then I'd rush to make up the work to get my grade back up.

If your OCD is slowing you down, talk to your parents and your teachers (or have your mom or dad join you to talk to your teachers). No one can help you if they don't know what's going on and why you aren't doing as well as they expect you to. Chances are good that you can all agree on a plan so you can learn and succeed in your own way, until you are more able to cope with your OCD and it doesn't interfere as much.

Your parents can also request a meeting with a school counselor, and accommodations can be made under a Section 504 plan, which provides intervention when a mental health disorder such as OCD interferes with school functioning.

College counselors can help, too, and you can talk to your professors about how you can meet deadlines—education is not one-size-fits-all, and in college this is especially true. Maybe you work better when you have several small goals to meet rather than just one looming deadline at the end of a semester. Don't be afraid to speak up—this is your life and your education and you have to make it work for you.

If your OCD symptoms are affecting your work, talk to your immediate supervisor as soon as possible. You're more likely to find a good solution than if you wait until the situation gets worse and your boss comes to you. Keeping it to yourself will do more damage than being upfront.

You may also have a legal right to request reasonable accommodations on the job. This is like providing an ergonomic keyboard for someone with carpal tunnel syndrome or allowing a person with a back condition to get up and walk around every 15 minutes, but it's tailor-made for you and your OCD symptoms. However, not all employers will be sympathetic to your concerns. For more information, check out "Entering the World of Work: What Youth with Mental Health Needs Should Know About Accommodations (see page 130)."

KEEPING REALISTIC EXPECTATIONS

I have my obsessions under control now. But that doesn't mean I don't still have bad thoughts. It's all about how we react to them—it's not about whether we have them at all or not at all. Remember, *everyone* has bad thoughts now and then: your favorite coach, your grandma, your second-grade teacher, even your dog if he could think the same way we do. (Wait, no. Dogs are pretty much the best, right?) Anyway, we all have bad thoughts, OCD or not, but we don't all panic upon having them. That is why we need to retrain our brains. If we didn't have OCD, we would still have the thoughts now and then, but we'd be more okay with them. That's the only difference.

When I was first diagnosed with OCD and my psychiatrist recommended *The Imp of the Mind* to me, I asked Peter to read it. Afterward he told me he's had bad thoughts like that too, like standing near the edge of a steep drop and thinking about stepping out. When Peter joined me on my next visit with my psychiatrist, Dr. Grant thanked him for saying that. That's really when I learned that most people have bad thoughts now and then, but they are able to write them off as meaningless and continue with their day with no guilt.

Overcoming OCD or even feeling better doesn't happen overnight. Don't expect perfection or a 100 percent, all-of-the-time recovery. If you do, you're bound to be disappointed and you may feel discouraged and like you may as well give up.

Have you ever vowed to break a bad habit, like wasting time on the Internet? You know you spend too much time watching dumb cat videos and making your own memes and not enough time doing homework, hanging out with your family, or talking to your friends in *real* life. So you promise yourself that you'll never look at another cat video again, you'll hang up your meme-creating hat, and you'll quit Facebook, once and for all.

I think we've all made resolutions like this at one point or another, and they never work because they're too strict. Cutting back on screen time, getting outside more, and, yes, obsessing less and performing fewer compulsions should be lifelong goals and routines. No one can be perfect all the time (or any of the time), and living with a black-and-white mentality is counterproductive. One week I was really busy and didn't make it to the gym. I felt discouraged and overwhelmed, like I'd have to start all over the next week because I'd somehow undone all of the progress I'd made. But of course that wasn't the case. I had built a routine and it wasn't that hard to get back into it. Even if you take a couple (or several) steps back, start again with one step forward. Maybe it's been several days since you've checked to make sure the oven is off before you leave home, but then one day you can't seem to stop. Don't throw up your hands in defeat and give up—wake up the next day with a new goal: *I won't check the oven before 8:00.* At 8:00, set the next goal: *I won't check the oven before 9:00.*

Although you want to feel better because OCD can make you pretty miserable, "recovery" is not a race. It's the training leading up to a race, the daily practice, the healthy habits, the getting out of bed even when it's the last thing you want to do. It takes determination. It's hard, but it's so worth it. Consider a less obsession-filled life your gold medal. I'll be in the stands, cheering you on! Maybe even wearing face paint.

Believe me, I get how hard it is. I still worry when I'm at a stoplight or stop sign right in front of a pedestrian that my foot will fall off the brake and I'll hit the person. But I get through these moments and move on, knowing deep down (sometimes it feels like the knowledge is *really* deep down) that if I don't want to hurt someone I won't. I rely on my coping skills and positive self-talk to move past each and every hint at a growing obsession.

LOOKING BACK

When I started writing this book I went back to read the books that helped me when I was first diagnosed with OCD. The one that I related to the most was *The Imp of the Mind* by Lee Baer because it was about "bad thoughts," the type of obsessions I was struggling with the most. Maybe it was late and I was tired, but reading that book again after all this time felt really emotional. I read those case histories and real-life examples of people who shared their deepest, most shameful secrets with Dr. Baer, and I felt so incredibly grateful for their courage. When I first visited Dr. Grant, I could barely sputter out a few words, and these people were explicit in a way that got me through some really dark times. If that guy could think *that* and Dr. Baer wasn't shocked or appalled, and Dr. Baer actually *helped* that guy, then there was hope for me, too.

Reading the book again after so many years drove home how happy I am now and how far I've come.

I still get choked up when I read or hear about other people's OCD. I cry because I feel terrible for the people who have struggled with obsessions. And I cry happy tears because the stories are reminders that I am truly not alone—not even close to it. Sometimes I feel a slight twinge of sadness and regret over how many years I was tormented before I finally got help, and the what-ifs and if-onlys this brought to mind. *If only I had known before . . .*

But I know now, and I hope you do, too. We are not alone.

Some of these psychiatrists, like Baer and Grant, have heard it all. I bet they've heard some variation of your obsession before, no matter how "out there" you think it is. Of course, they feel their patients' pain. Sure, it may be true that there are others like us, but that doesn't make it *easy* to get better, to get past the painful parts and to the good stuff. We all have to take our own individual journeys toward wellness. The good news is we don't have to take them alone.

LOOKING AHEAD

Although I once hoped I would never, ever have a bad thought again, that wasn't a reasonable goal to set. The goal *cannot* be never to have a weird, bad, or scary thought again. You are not a robot. You are a human being, and you *will* think another bad thought. Irrational fears will seep in. You can count on that. The goal must be to obsess less and not let obsessions or compulsions control you. The goal must be not to freak out when a bad thought or fear pops into your head.

I retrained my brain. You can too. It's not so much mind over matter as it is mind over mind. Fighting fire with fire. When you obsess, your mind is going against your wishes, and your instinct to push the obsession away is normal but ineffective.

The way I see it, there are a few different ways to respond to an unwanted "bad" thought:

1. Panic, sweat, berate yourself, cry, and pull at your hair, causing a snowball effect, leading you to believe you are a bad person for thinking a bad thought.

2. Enjoy it. Love it. Keep thinking about it and taking pleasure in it. Fantasize about it. Carry it out!

3. Think, "Dude, that was messed up. Ha!" Move on, never think of it again. React the same way with the next weird or bad thought.

The first response is probably pretty typical of someone with OCD. The second response is more typical of a person who doesn't have OCD but has some other mental disorder, someone who *will* do something wrong, illegal, immoral, and so on.

Work toward achieving the third response, whether you struggle with bad thoughts or phobias like a fear of contamination, losing control, or being responsible for something terrible happening. You might not say "Dude," but the gist of the desired response is that you should care a whole lot less about those strange things that enter your mind, as long as you realize they aren't cool or rational. Let them go—don't dwell on them, hating that you thought those things. If you have OCD, you don't have to worry about swinging all the way to the other side, of becoming the type of person who carries out bad thoughts. You can just concentrate on retraining your brain to have a more relaxed response to your obsessions, including bad thoughts.

Try telling yourself, "That's just my OCD trying to boss me around again. I don't have to listen." It can help you remember that it's not the "real you" that's creating the obsessive thoughts—it's your OCD.

Facing your worst fear is healthy. Acting on an unpleasant thought, like the idea of leaving home without checking the lock

50 times, is part of exposure and response prevention therapy. You *should* leave without checking the lock over and over again, and doing so will be awfully uncomfortable at first. But you can get through it. That uncomfortable feeling is temporary, and the tradeoff is so worth it: a life with less anxiety and more joy. A life *you* are in control of, not OCD.

Not long after I met Dr. Grant for the first time I set a pretty arbitrary goal: I was going to be happy by my birthday. It was two months away—what a tall order! When May 17 rolled around, I *was* happier. I had fully adjusted to my medication, I had had great visits with Dr. Grant, and everyone who really mattered to me knew I had OCD. I rang in my 27th birthday with Peter, my brothers, and all of my friends—I had never had them all in the same room before! I ordered pancakes for dinner and laughed all night, opening gifts and dropping hints about marriage to Peter.

A few months later Peter and I spent a long weekend on Lake Superior. We rented bikes and planned to ride around an island for the day. I realized I hadn't packed the right clothes for the weather, so we popped into a local shop so I could get a long-sleeve T-shirt. After browsing for a few minutes I found the perfect one: It was green, my favorite color, and it had a little burst of sunshine and the words "Life is good" on the front. Earlier that year the message would have seemed like a cruel joke. But now life *was* good. It was so good. And I owed it to finally reaching out and getting the help I needed. To taking those first terrifying steps toward recovery and plugging away at it, day by day. My friend who called me Ali Sunshine was right—I'm an optimistic person, even with an anxiety disorder. After struggling for so many years I was *me*, the person I had always wanted to be on the inside and out.

I still wear that shirt, eight years later. Life is still good. Some days when I pull it on over my head I think about how it felt to buy it. Other days I think nothing of it, other than it's gotten a little tighter and, man, I've had this shirt a long time—because having a good, relatively obsession-free life is pretty standard now.

Peter heard the hints I dropped at my birthday dinner, loud and clear. A little over a year later we got married. We each chose a song that meant something to us and our relationship and asked a friend to read it at our wedding. Peter chose "Something Changed" by Pulp, and I chose "Push" by Sarah McLachlan. I asked my friend Lauren to do the honor.

When Lauren spoke the line "You make me feel less crazy when otherwise I'd drown," I began to cry. Yeah, I know "crazy" isn't the PC term, but I really had felt crazy at times and Peter really did make me feel less so. I squeezed his hand—the hand that would soon be adorned with a wedding band, the hand that belonged to the man I loved more than I had ever hoped I could love anyone, the man who knew damn near everything about me and was comfortable saying things like "You're not going to go crazy if you don't have that pill, are you?" after I dropped one on the floor of my car, or "I'll follow you wherever you go," meaning that no matter how low I may get he will never leave me or give up on me.

I didn't know if I would ever stop obsessing, but I have come really far, with mostly good days and some bad days—but for the most part the bad days are typical bad days, not "OCD bad days." I have forgiven myself for the obsessions I've already had, and even for the obsessive thoughts that will pop into my head in the future.

I have the benefit of being in my 30s—I can look back in time, sometimes by several years, think of the really, really bad times, and know that I came out of them with some tiny battle scars that serve as hopeful reminders of my strength. I know now that even if I get depressed again or find myself in an obsessive loop, I have the tools to get out of it again. I won't ever give up, and I don't want you to ever give up, either. Promise me you won't.

You have what it takes to feel better. No one is perfect. No one goes through life without a few bumps in the road, and even if you've come across some really big bumps, keep fighting. You are worth it! You can be who you are, who you were *meant to be*. You can be your*self*—with OCD.

REFERENCES AND RESOURCES

Allen, Hannah. *A Narrative of God's Gracious Dealings with that Choice Christian Mrs. Hannah Allen* (London: Printed by John Wallis, 1683). An autobiography about a woman's struggle with obsessive thoughts and how her doctor tried to treat them.

Baer, Lee. *Getting Control: Overcoming Your Obsessions and Compulsions* (New York: Penguin Plume, 2012). As the subtitle implies, it's a how-to guide on dealing with obsessions and compulsions and contains helpful checklists and coping techniques.

Baer, Lee. *The Imp of the Mind: Exploring the Silent Epidemic of Obsessive Bad Thoughts* (New York: Penguin Plume, 2001). This book helped me tremendously, because its primary focus is on the same "bad thoughts" I struggled with for so many years. It's packed with case studies and examples of bad thoughts other people worked hard to overcome.

Bell, Jeff. *Rewind, Replay, Repeat: A Memoir of Obsessive-Compulsive Disorder* (Center City, MN: Hazelden, 2007). A memoir about Bell's life with OCD and his attempts to overcome his constant worrying, rechecking, and persistent intrusive thoughts.

The Book of Margery Kempe, a Modern Version by W. Butler-Bowdon (London: Jonathan Cape, 1936 [originally 1436]), pp. 352–3. An early book that was likely describing OCD, as experienced by a woman named Margery Kempe.

Diagnostic and Statistical Manual of Mental Disorders (DSM), 5th Edition (Arlington, VA: American Psychiatric Publishing, 2013). The "bible" of psychiatric disorders and diagnoses, this comprehensive resource helps psychologists, counselors, nurses, occupational and rehabilitation therapists, social workers, and forensic and legal specialists make diagnoses and craft treatment plans.

Drake, Victoria J. "Micronutrients and Cognitive Function." *Linus Pauling Institute Research Newsletter,* Spring-Summer 2011. Accessed September 9, 2013. lpi.oregonstate.edu/ss11/cognitive.html

"Entering the World of Work: What Youth with Mental Health Needs Should Know About Accommodations." United States Department of Labor, Office of Disability Employment Policy. www.dol.gov/odep/pubs/fact/transitioning.htm

Foa, Edna B., and Reid Wilson. *Stop Obsessing! How to Overcome Your Obsessions and Compulsions* (New York: Bantam, 2001). This practical book has step-by-step programs for overcoming obsessions and compulsions, charts and guides, questionnaires, and tips on how to find a therapist.

Got OCD? A Guide for Teens (Chicago, IL: OCD Chicago, 2009). Find the pamphlet at OCD Education Station (ocdeducationstation.org). www.ocdeducationstation.org/images/uploads/guides/got-ocd.pdf

Herkewitz, William. "The Glow From Your Gadgets Is Disrupting Your Sleep Cycle." *Popular Mechanics,* August 1, 2013.

"Howie Mandel on Living with OCD," *Larry King Now,* December 10, 2012. Howie Mandel discusses his struggle with OCD and ADHD, describing how he tried to downplay how difficult his symptoms made his life. Access at www.ora.tv/larrykingnow.

"How to Choose a Behavior Therapist" by Michael Jenike, M.D. In Wilhelm, S., and G.S. Steketee, *Cognitive Therapy for Obsessive-Compulsive Disorder: A Guide for Professionals* (Oakland, CA: New Harbinger Publications, 2006).

Hyman, Bruce M., and Cherry Pedrick. *The OCD Workbook: Your Guide to Breaking Free from Obsessive-Compulsive Disorder* (Oakland, CA: New Harbinger Publications, 2010). This practical workbook includes self-assessment tools, information about medication, and advice on finding the right professional help.

Kantermann, Thomas. "Circadian Biology: Sleep-Styles Shaped by Light-Styles." *Current Biology*, vol. 23, no. 16, 19 August 2013, 689–690.

Ma, Michael Yiran. "OCD: An Analysis of Clinical Obsessive-Compulsive Disorder in Modern Society." *Vanderbilt Undergraduate*

Research Journal, vol. 4, 2008. This paper examines current OCD research, attempts to debunk inaccurate media portrayals of the disorder, describes possible causes of OCD, and discusses effective treatment methods.

Mandel, Howie. *Here's the Deal: Don't Touch Me* (New York: Bantam Books, 2009). Mandel discusses his journey with OCD in this autobiography, as well as funny anecdotes and personal stories.

March, John S., with Christine M. Benton. *Talking Back to OCD: The Program That Helps Kids and Teens Say "No Way"—and Parents Say "Way to Go"* (New York: Guilford Press, 2007). Details the doctor's eight-step program to help teens combat OCD, as well as a section especially for parents. Some of the tips include creating a nickname for OCD as a reminder that the reader isn't the disorder; making a symptom chart; and breaking the "rules" about performing rituals.

Mayo Clinic Staff. "Depression and Anxiety: Exercise Eases Symptoms." Mayo Foundation for Medical Education and Research (MFMER), 2011. Accessed September 9, 2013. www.mayoclinic.com/health/depression-and-exercise/MH00043

Mayo Clinic Staff. "Exercise: 7 Benefits of Regular Physical Activity." Mayo Foundation for Medical Education and Research (MFMER), 2011. Accessed September 9, 2013. www.mayoclinic.com/health/exercise/HQ01676

Moore, John. *Of Religious Melancholy: A Sermon Preach'd before the Queen at White-Hall, March the 6th, 1691/2* (London: Printed for William Rogers, 1692), pp. 19–27. First a sermon about unwanted "naughty" thoughts and then published as a pamphlet, this early book about unwanted obsessive thoughts had seven editions between 1692 and 1708.

"PANDAS: Frequently Asked Questions About Pediatric Autoimmune Neuropsychiatric Disorders Associated with Streptococcal Infections." National Institute of Mental Health. Accessed September 8, 2013. www.nimh.nih.gov/health/publications/pandas/index.shtml

Ross, Carolyn Coker. "Healthy Gut, Healthy Mind: 5 Foods to Improve Mental Health." *Psychology Today,* January 29, 2013.

Ruscio A.M., D.J. Stein, W.T. Chiu, and R.C. Kessler. "The Epidemiology of Obsessive-Compulsive Disorder in the National Comorbidity Survey Replication." *Molecular Psychiatry*, August 26, 2008.

Shy, Shannon. *It'll Be Okay: How I Kept OCD from Ruining My Life* (Bloomington, IN: AuthorHouse, 2009). Shy details how he overcame OCD using practical techniques, which he shares with his readers, as well as inspirational advice.

"Vitamin B6 (pyridoxine)." National Standard Research Collaboration, 2012. Accessed at Mayo Clinic website September 9, 2013. www.mayoclinic.com/health/vitamin-b6/NS_patient-b6

Zeratsky, Katherine. "Can a Junk Food Diet Increase Your Risk of Depression?" Mayo Foundation for Medical Education and Research (MFMER), 2012. Accessed September 9, 2013. www.mayoclinic.com/health/depression-and-diet/AN02057

International OCD Foundation
OCfoundation.org
Founded by a group of people with OCD in 1986, the International OCD Foundation (IOCDF) is an international nonprofit organization made up of people with obsessive-compulsive disorder (OCD) and related disorders, as well as their families, friends, professionals and others. The site includes a list of resources, extensive information about OCD, a provider database, and more.

Machine Man website
machinemanthemovie.com
Learn more about OCD from others and share your own art, writing, and other creative work about your experience with the disorder. The goal of the Machine Man website is to not only increase general awareness of OCD but also to raise money for *Machine Man,* a movie about what it's like to live with OCD.

Peace of Mind Foundation
peaceofmind.com
The Peace of Mind Foundation was created by Elizabeth McIngvale, the first national spokesperson for the International OCD Foundation. Visit the website to learn about Elizabeth's own struggle with OCD, the many different forms OCD can take, and how to find a treatment provider and support group. You can also view video podcasts and take the OCD Challenge.

ACKNOWLEDGMENTS

My name may be on the cover of this book, but I didn't write it alone.

Judy Galbraith, thank you for agreeing to publish *Being Me with OCD*. You helped me realize a lifelong dream to be an author, and I feel doubly blessed because my first book enables me to help others. I'm passionate about writing *and* reducing the stigma around mental illness, so this is the best of both worlds. I am so grateful.

Eric Braun—where do I begin? When I mentioned at an impromptu gathering that I have OCD and liked to write personal essays about it, you encouraged me to propose a book to Free Spirit. You sat down with the acquisitions editor and me to go over ideas, you read my proposal before I turned it in, you agreed to stay on as my editor even when life handed you a hugely exciting opportunity—and, most of all, you empowered me to write candidly about my obsessions because you knew it would help my readers. Thank you for weeding through my rough first draft and organizing it, and for continuing to help me long after you *had* to. You earned my trust and pushed me to do more than I thought I could, and I can never thank you enough for that.

Tasha Kenyon, thank you for your beautiful design work. I typed this book into a boring black-and-white document, and your creative, colorful, and practical layout brought my words to life.

Margie Lisovskis, thank you for bringing my book to completion and asking thoughtful questions to fine-tune sensitive details. Elena Meredith, thank you for starting off as my publicist and getting my first "OCD essay" published, and Anastasia Scott, thanks for taking the reins, coming up with plans I never knew existed, and for reading my many emails! Thanks to everyone else at Free Spirit who had a hand in making this book a reality: Darsi for your copyediting and production editing expertise; Penne and Lindsey and everyone in sales; Steven for overseeing the design.

Aimee Jackson, thank you for helping me get this idea off the ground and for believing in its potential as a book for teens and young adults who needed a book just for them.

Elizabeth McIngvale, thank you for writing the foreword and for your valuable feedback. Your support means the world to me.

To the teens and young adults who contributed essays: Thank you for sharing your personal experiences with me and the readers of *Being Me with OCD*. This book wouldn't be complete without your stories of struggle and triumph, of confusion and awareness, of fear and courage. You took time out of your busy school and work schedules to help others with OCD. I thank you, and I know my readers will, too.

James J. Crist, thank you for giving my book an expert review, particularly the sections with all of those big scientific words and confusing concepts.

Dr. Jon Grant: Thank you for saving my life.

Alison Behnke, thanks for agreeing to writing dates to keep me going and for always listening, even via email.

Amanda Bacon Dwinell, thank you for letting me write about you and the details of our friendship so that I could illustrate what a strong support system looks like.

Eli and Asher, I love you. I'm thanking you now for something you won't understand for years. The light and joy you've brought to my life are worthy of an ode.

Mom and Dad: People say that parents learn how to raise their kids as they go along. You must have had a brood of children in another life because you did everything right in my eyes. I wouldn't be a writer today if you hadn't let me be a voracious reader as a kid, even when you wished I'd put down my book to gaze out the window at beautiful scenery, engage in dinner conversation, or turn out the lights and go to sleep—and turn off that flashlight under the covers, too!

Peter Dotson, thank you for everything. For letting me be who I am, which can't always be easy, for encouraging me to write, and for being truly excited about this book. Thanks for saying, "Sure, why not?" when I asked if I could write about you and our relationship and the conversations you surely assumed would stay private. Thank you for being unfazed when I told you I was diagnosed with OCD, for reading about the disorder when I've asked you to, and for caring about my feelings without treating me like a fragile object. I'm so lucky to be your wife.

INDEX

ABOUT THE AUTHOR

Alison Dotson is a writer, copyeditor, and proof-reader who was diagnosed with OCD at age 26, after suffering from "taboo" obsessions for nearly two decades. Today, she still has occasional bad thoughts, but she knows how to deal with them in healthy ways. Alison is the president of OCD Twin Cities, an affiliate of the International OCD Foundation. She lives in Minneapolis, Minnesota, with her husband and two rescue dogs, Tuffy and Gracie.

Other Great Books from Free Spirit

ADHD in HD
Brains Gone Wild
by Jonathan Chesner

A kinetic collection of frank personal stories of failure and success, hilarious anecdotes, wild ideas, and blunt advice that will resonate with teens and young adults.
160 pp.; softcover; 2-color; illust.; 6" x 7½"

When Nothing Matters Anymore
(Revised & Updated Edition)
A Survival Guide for Depressed Teens
by Bev Cobain, R.N.,C.

Full of solid information and straight talk, *When Nothing Matters Anymore* defines and explains adolescent depression, reveals how common it is, describes the symptoms, and spreads the good news that depression is treatable.
176 pp.; softcover; illust.; 6" x 9"

The Power to Prevent Suicide
(Updated Edition)
A Guide for Teens Helping Teens
by Richard E. Nelson, Ph.D., Judith C. Galas, foreword by Bev Cobain, R.N.,C.

Suicide prevention is possible if you know the signs. Updated with new facts, statistics, and resources, this book gives teens the information and insight they need to recognize the risk and respond appropriately.
128 pp.; softcover; illust.; 6" x 9"

Fighting Invisible Tigers
Stress Management for Teens
by Earl Hipp

This book offers proven techniques that teens can use to deal with stressful situations in school, at home, and among friends. Filled with interesting facts, student quotes, and fun activities, this book is a great resource for any teen who's said, "I'm stressed out!"
144 pp.; softcover; 2-color; illust.; 6" x 9"

Words Wound
Delete Cyberbullying and Make Kindness Go Viral
by Justin W. Patchin, Ph.D., and Sameer Hinduja, Ph.D.

Written by experts in cyberbullying prevention and reviewed by teens, this book provides strategies for dealing with teenage bullying happening online. It also presents ways for teens to make their schools and their communities kinder places that are free from online cruelty.
200 pp.; softcover; 2-color; 6" x 7½"

Interested in purchasing multiple quantities and receiving volume discounts?
Contact edsales@freespirit.com or call 1.800.735.7323 and ask for Education Sales.

Many Free Spirit authors are available for speaking engagements, workshops, and keynotes. Contact speakers@freespirit.com or call 1.800.735.7323.

For pricing information, to place an order, or to request a free catalog, contact:

Free Spirit Publishing Inc.
800.735.7323 • help4kids@freespirit.com • www.freespirit.com